The English Revolution

1600–1660

Essays edited by

E. W. IVES

Lecturer in Modern History, University of Birmingham

EDWARD ARNOLD

© Edward Arnold (Publishers) Ltd 1968

First Published 1968 by
Edward Arnold (Publishers) Ltd
41 Maddox Street, London W1

Boards edition SBN: 7131 5426 8
Paper edition SBN: 7131 5427 6

Printed in Great Britain by
W & J Mackay & Co Ltd, Chatham, Kent

Preface

The essays in this collection had their origin in a series of talks broadcast by the B.B.C., early in 1966, under the title 'The English Revolution'. The series attempted to show the connexion between society and politics in the first sixty years of the seventeenth century, by studying different social units and groups.

Eight of the essays which follow are, in substance and form, the original scripts. The copious quotation from contemporary sources originally included has been somewhat reduced, and additional explanatory matter has been added where necessary, but otherwise a minimum of alteration has been made, and there has been no attempt to transform the scripts into academic papers. For this reason, there are no critical footnotes; full references are, however, given to the quotations which have normally been modernized.

Of the two remaining essays, the introduction by Professor Austin Woolrych has been specially written for this volume. Dr. Brian Manning's essay on the Levellers replaces the dramatization of the Putney Debates which he contributed to the broadcast series, and which was not suitable for printing in essay form.

The authors would like to pay tribute to the Further Education Department of the B.B.C. for its imaginative conception of this series, and particularly to Mr. Howard Smith and Mr. Adrian Johnson who produced the series. In reissuing the talks in a more permanent form, it is hoped to provide a useful introduction to the social context of the English Civil War, not only for students in the universities and higher forms in schools, but also for the lay public interested in the period. For this reason a select bibliography is appended, and each essay concludes with a suggestion for further reading.

Contents

The Contributors

Alan Everitt	Professor of English Local History in the University of Leicester
F. J. Fisher	Professor of Economic History at the London School of Economics in the University of London
E. W. Ives	Lecturer in Modern History in the University of Birmingham
H. F. Kearney	Reader in History in the University of Sussex
Brian Manning	Lecturer in History in the University of Manchester
D. H. Pennington	Fellow of Balliol College, Oxford
Ivan Roots	Professor of Modern History in the University of Exeter
Barry Supple	Professor of Economic and Social History in the University of Sussex
Austin Woolrych	Professor of History in the University of Lancaster

The English Revolution: an introduction

AUSTIN WOOLRYCH

I

A generation ago it would not have seemed too difficult to write a concise introductory essay on what the English Revolution was about and what happened in it. Samuel Rawson Gardiner's great histories had mapped it out so clearly; Sir Charles Firth had completed the work and presented the authorized version to a wider public in his justly famous biography of Cromwell. Building on their foundations, the young George Macaulay Trevelyan produced, in *England under the Stuarts*, an account brimful of the happy certainties of the Whig tradition. Firth passed the mantle to Godfrey Davies, whose volume in the *Oxford History of England*, published in 1937, was still in most respects an epitome of Gardiner's eighteen volumes.

Today it all looks different, and no major event in our history is more hedged about with question-marks than the Great Rebellion. This is not because the older historians were necessarily wrong, in any simple sense. The factual accuracy of Gardiner and Firth is generally as remarkable as the heroic scale of their researches. It is rather that we are no longer fully satisfied with the kind of explanations that they offered, or with the limited area of national politics on which they mainly concentrated. We have learned to ask new questions of the past, and the contributions to this book indicate some of the lines of inquiry that historians are currently pursuing. A tardy awareness of developments in the social sciences has led us to broaden the scope of historical studies and enlarge our notions of historical causation. Whatever we personally think of the doctrines of Karl Marx and Max Weber, to name only two giants, their shadows and many others fall inevitably across our pages. Even sixth-formers seem to be expected nowadays to have their views, for example, on how to interpret the rise of the gentry and the relationship between Puritanism and capitalism.

As the dust began to settle on those particular battlefields, we were left realizing how little we still knew about the distribution of wealth and power in Stuart England, or about the relations between economic circumstances and political and religious attitudes. We are emerging, a little clearer-eyed, from a period of grand speculation and hypothesis in seventeenth-century studies. The value of the hypotheses—especially those about the rising or declining fortunes of the gentry and their effects on political allegiance—may ultimately be seen to lie less in their intrinsic validity than in the stimulus they have given to a mass of more detailed and more disciplined research. They helped to show that we can best advance knowledge now by close and quantitative investigation of particular counties, particular institutions or particular social groups. Historians have grown wary of generalizing about England as though it were a homogeneous community; they take fuller account now of the fact that when a gentleman three hundred years ago spoke of his 'country' he meant his county. They see England more realistically as the sum of her many county communities, each an important unit of government, each an arena in which the gentlefolk lived out their social lives and fought out their social rivalries, each inclined to put local interests before national, and in their sum exhibiting a great variety in social make-up and political attitudes.

It is symptomatic that the next three chapters of this book are all concerned with different aspects of the county community, and the one after with that very special community the City of London. Three more contributions, dealing with Puritans, scientists and lawyers, reflect current interest in the intellectual roots from which the makers of the English Revolution may have drawn sustenance. The lawyers constituted a distinct social 'interest' whose attitude mattered greatly as the conflict deepened between the court and the political nation at large; so did the merchants, who are shown in another chapter to have been a far from simple, monolithic grouping. Finally an account of the Levellers illustrates the cataclysmic change that came over the climate of political discussion when, in the aftermath of civil war, the small ruling segment of society was challenged from below.

What would have struck an older historian about this collection is the absence of any special treatment of the constitutional issues and the immediate political conflicts that gave rise to civil war. About these there is less that is new to be said, and since the main purpose of this introduction is to sketch a chronological framework for the more specialized contributions that follow, it is here that the more familiar aspects of the course of events will be briefly treated. But before that something more difficult must be attempted, and that is a swift impression of the kind of society in which the political, social and intellectual conflicts of the English Revolution were generated. In their original form as broadcast talks, the discussions in this book alternated with a parallel series by Mr. Peter Laslett on the structure of early Stuart society and the kinds of conflict to which it was susceptible. The next few pages make no attempt to summarize the rich content of his contribution. They simply sketch some of the more obvious facts of social life in Stuart England and try to convey some idea of how government was related to society.

We can best begin, perhaps, by picturing a population less than a tenth as large as that of today and comprising an overwhelming majority of country-dwellers. Out of perhaps four and a half million people in England and Wales, about a quarter of a million lived in London. But London differed in scale from all other towns far more greatly than now. Only a small handful of provincial towns topped the ten thousand mark, and about six Englishmen out of seven lived in communities of less than a thousand souls. There was no mass-association of people in similar jobs such as modern industry and modern urban society provide, and there was therefore no framework in which class-consciousness as we know it today could form itself. The typical community was the village; the commonest occupation small-scale husbandry; the essential social unit the family. Society was a hierarchy, ranging from great nobles down to cottagers and paupers. Before the revolution brought all in doubt, people accepted the fact of social subordination, of differences of degree, and their preachers constantly told them (as Shakespeare had done) that it was part of the divine order of things. For most men, their relations of dependence upon those just above them in the local community and of influence over those just below them mattered much more than any notion of a common class interest with others of the same kind of occupation and income-level in other communities. This is one reason why interpretations of the English Revolution based on modern concepts of class are apt to look anachronistic.

In a society dominated by status rather than class, the crucial dividing line ran between the small minority who could style themselves gentlemen (or above) and the large majority who could not. Perhaps one in twenty-five of the population belonged to families in the former category. Below that level, men might become constables, parish clerks, churchwardens or possibly overseers of the poor, but their small authority would scarcely stir a ripple beyond the bounds of their village. Those who happened to hold freehold land worth forty shillings a year might cast a vote in a parliamentary election, but these were rare occasions and only quite exceptionally involved any judgment upon national political issues. The great majority of the people lay not only below the level of political participation but below that of political consciousness as well. When the events of the Civil War threatened to change this state of affairs and prompted questions such as the Levellers and Agitators raised at Putney, most members of the ruling class felt that the tide of revolution was carrying them a great deal too far.

Even if we think of this ruling segment as numbering about one twenty-fifth of the whole people we may tend to exaggerate its size. Women were not expected to concern themselves with politics. Moreover it was land more than any other form of wealth that gave a man status and political weight, and the number of landowners substantial enough to affect decision-making at either national or county level was not very large. Professor Aylmer has attempted a rough count based on the year 1633, his figures inevitably becoming less definite as he moves down the scale.[1] There were then 122

[1] G. E. Aylmer, *The King's Servants: the Civil Service of Charles I* (1961), p. 331.

English peers, twenty-six bishops, and slightly over 300 in a group just below the peerage which included the eldest sons of peers, Englishmen holding Scottish or Irish titles, and the new order of baronets. Then came between 1,500 and 1,800 knights, 7,000—9,000 esquires and 10,000—14,000 mere 'gentlemen'. The last category comprised the lesser landed gentry and many whose status derived not primarily from land but from commercial wealth, professional or academic standing or office under the crown. As a body they were rather on the fringe of the ruling class. It was the ten thousand or so men ranked as esquire or above who really counted politically. It was from their ranks that most of the important county offices were filled—lord lieutenant, deputy lieutenant, sheriff, justice of the peace and so on. They furnished most of the king's servants, the men who mattered in the central administration and the royal household. They took most of the seats in the House of Commons. The higher one goes in the social scale, the larger the proportion of men in each category that one finds actively engaged in national or local politics.

It was a small enough ruling class to be quite close-knit, especially within each county community. Yet as ruling classes went in the monarchies of that time it was reasonably broad, and compared with its counterparts in (say) France or Spain it was much more politically aware and politically responsible. This was partly because English kings had never been rich enough, even if they had felt the need, to erect a bureaucratic local government of professional, salaried officials. They relied on the unpaid services of the peers and leading gentry in the counties and of the most substantial citizens in the corporate towns. The heads of the leading county families executed ordinary justice upon malefactors in their quarter sessions, supervised a wide range of local administration, enforced with varying degrees of zeal a host of statutes, collected the subsidies that parliament voted, mustered the militia—the catalogue could go on a long way. In Stuart England most government was necessarily local government, and the county provided its essential framework. The great problem, as Professor Roots shows in the next chapter, was for central government to secure collaboration from the county communities; the Great Rebellion marked its crucial failure. Professor Everitt further illustrates how assertive and unco-operative the counties could be, and Mr. Pennington shows how the coming of civil war increased rather than lessened the dependence of England's new masters on the local communities.

The social structure of the English landed classes differed from that of their continental counterparts in one way which had had very important consequences for the development of parliament: only a small élite among them enjoyed the status and privileges of nobility. Elsewhere in Europe, most substantial landowners were noblemen, and newcomers to the land from the ranks of the bourgeoisie sought to acquire noble titles and privileges as soon as possible. The great social divide was between nobleman and commoner, and this was reflected in the composition of national representative assemblies, where they survived. These had most commonly comprised the three separate orders of clergy, nobles and commoners (or third estate), and in many lands they had been weakened by the built-in antagonism between noble landlords and bourgeois traders or officials. There had been various outcomes: total atrophy (as in the French Estates-General), the withdrawal of the nobles and clergy, leaving only a few impotent representatives of the towns (as in Castile), the tyranny of the landowners over the bourgeoisie (as in Brandenburg and Prussia), or in the unique case of the Dutch Republic the ascendancy of an urban patriciate. Even where the estates preserved a reasonable balance between aristocratic and bourgeois interests (as in Saxony or Aragon), they hardly shared the vitality of the English parliament.

In England the titled nobility were remarkably few. There were only fifty-five English peers in 1603, and no more than 121 in 1641. Professor Lawrence Stone has recently argued that they suffered a serious though temporary fall in power and prestige under the early Stuarts.[2] Although they largely recovered from the financial crisis that had affected most of them in the later sixteenth century, their military power had largely gone, their holdings of land (and hence their territorial influence) were much depleted, their economic recovery was too often at their tenants' expense, their rank was cheapened because the Stuarts sold noble titles for cash, and many of

[2] Lawrence Stone, *The Crisis of the Aristocracy 1558-1641* (1964).

them became absentee landlords, resident at and dependent on a hated royal court. The great bulk of substantial landowners were not nobles but gentry: baronets, knights, esquires and gentlemen. The relative decline of the titled aristocracy gave this squirearchy a greater political and social influence than ever. But proud as the gentry were of their status, in law they were commoners, and they lacked the essential noble privileges that their French or Spanish equivalents enjoyed. The line that divided gentlemen from the social orders below them was an important one, but it was not so exactly drawn as in the continental monarchies, nor did it mark so deep a fissure. Entry into the ranks of the gentry from below required no royal patent, and a coat of arms could be had for a price. Knights and gentlemen could engage in commercial or industrial enterprises without loss of caste, they intermarried with wealthy burgher families relatively freely, and they often apprenticed their younger sons to the better trades.

Above all, if they wished to serve in parliament they had to seek election to the House of Commons. There was thus no serious clash of social interest between the two Houses, for the richest knights of the shire in the Commons rivalled not a few of the Lords in wealth, and many a peer's son sat in the lower house—forty-eight in the Long Parliament, for example. In the Commons, landed gentlemen and rich citizens sat together, though in very unequal proportions. Legally the Long Parliament should have contained just over four hundred resident burgesses and ninety knights of the shire—more than four townsmen to every one country gentlemen. In fact there were more than four landed gentlemen to every one genuine townsman, for the squires had been taking over the borough seats ever since the fifteenth century. Yet the House of Commons was a strikingly homogeneous body and it showed little tendency to split along class lines. So many great merchants had a foot on the land, so many landowners had a finger in commercial enterprise that no clear line separated them, and there was a further blurring because groups like the lawyers, the courtiers and the royal officials commonly had an interest in both town and country. The fifty or so merchants who sat in an average parliament were a respected body, but commercial wealth carried relatively less political weight than broad acres. If it

seems undervalued, however, one should remember how few Englishmen outside London were town-dwellers, and how readily
merchants who brought land—as they mostly did—acquired the
outlook and values of the landed gentry. The ruling class of Stuart
England was in a real sense a single class.

Another factor that strengthened this class in its solidarity against
any abuse of government was its veneration for the common law.
The Inns of Court were not only training-grounds for professional
lawyers but finishing schools for sons of the gentry who wanted no
more than a taste of the town and a bit of legal know-how to help
them manage their estates and hold up their heads among their
fellow justices. But the Inns left their stamp on many a parliament-
man—on nearly two-thirds of those originally elected to the Long
Parliament, for example. Dr. Ives describes later how prone they
were to reduce political or constitutional controversies to legal terms,
and how ominous it was when the common law, so lately a buttress
of the throne, came to be used to erode its foundations. Among the
intellectual forebears of the English Revolution none stands so high
as Sir Edward Coke.

II

If we are to sketch the sequence of developments that brought
England to the brink of revolution, the first problem is where to
begin in time. The conventional starting-point is 1603, the year
King James travelled south to take up the Tudor inheritance. In some
respects it is too late. The long rise in prices had already taken its toll
of the crown's revenue and the lands of the aristocracy; the exceptional mobility of noble and gentry estates was already rising towards
the peak it reached in the decade 1610–9. The squirearchy, long
indispensable in local government, had already consolidated their
hold on the House of Commons and explored there the techniques of
opposition. By the fifteen-nineties the great age of Tudor government was clearly passing and the standards of public morality among
the queen's servants were already slipping.[3]

[3] See J. E. Neale, 'The Elizabethan political scene', in *Essays in Elizabethan History* (1958).

Yet in other ways it is misleading to push the genesis of revolution back to 1603. For at least another quarter of a century no one aimed consciously at changing the basic structure of either government or society. King's servants, county magistrates and parliament-men alike sought only to preserve their time-honoured inheritance and hold in trim the precious balance between the crown's necessary prerogatives and the subject's lawful rights. Professor Everitt rightly emphasizes the conservatism of the representatives of the local communities, even when they came up all angry to the Long Parliament.[4] Nevertheless the advent of the Stuarts soon led to fresh tensions in the body politic, and is as good a point as any at which to take up the story.

The thirty-seven years that separate the general joy at James's accession from the general indignation of 1640 fall into four stages. The first spans the remaining life-time of the last of Elizabeth's great ministers, Robert Cecil, whom James made Earl of Salisbury. Until he died in 1612, Salisbury maintained something of Tudor competence in the royal administration, but his efforts were constantly undermined by the king. James was indolent and extravagant; worse, he looked upon the many offices in his gift less as places of public trust than as rewards to distribute among his friends. 'He did not choose men for his jobs, but bestowed jobs on his men.'[5] Thereby he not only accelerated the deterioration in the public service but alienated many of his English subjects, who could not bear to see so many coveted prizes go to Scotsmen and boon companions. The long first parliament of the reign, spanning nearly seven years, probed many issues that would lead to greater conflict later. Finance was prominent among them; resentment was growing against the king's feudal rights of wardship and purveyance, and the controversial impositions—additional import duties imposed by royal prerogative—started the Commons on their mounting opposition to the crown's powers of economic regulation. James by his tactlessness provoked more than one wrangle over the Commons' traditional privileges, he claiming that they depended on the favour of his grant, they retorting that their privileges were theirs by right. There were

[4] Below, p. 48.
[5] H. R. Trevor-Roper, 'King James and his bishops', *History Today*, v (1955), 573.

also disputes over religion. The Commons, baulked in their own attempts to initiate further reforms in the church, challenged the canons passed by convocation in 1604 and took up the cause of the Puritan ministers who were deprived of their livings under them. But this was border-skirmishing compared with what came later, and the Tudor framework of government still held.

The next stage takes us to 1621 and marks a further sharp decline in the quality of government. It was also a period of non-parliamentary rule, for in ten whole years after the dissolution of January 1611, there was only one brief and sterile parliament in 1614. For six years after Salisbury's death a faction led by the Howard clan dominated the king's counsels, and the royal service was steadily undermined by incompetence, corruption and extravagance. These were the years when James's flashy young favourites made their notorious careers out of his weakness; first Robert Carr, who rose to the earldom of Somerset, and then after Carr's scandalous downfall in 1615, George Villiers, created Earl and finally Duke of Buckingham. These were the years also when offices came to be bought and sold as never before, and by 1618 the whole royal patronage was virtually controlled by Buckingham, to his enormous profit. There was a brisk traffic in titles too. The new rank of baronet was created in 1611 simply to be sold, and the trade in peerages began four years later. When offices of state became the sport of minions and the kingdom's highest honours were put up for cash, a growing proportion of the nobility and gentry began to nurse a sense of outrage.

The conduct of national policy deepened their resentment. The Howards did all they could to align England with Spain, and even after Buckingham supplanted them, the man who most influenced James's foreign policy was Count Gondomar, the Spanish ambassador. When James took up the idea of marrying Prince Charles to a Spanish Infanta and increasingly relaxed the penal laws against the Roman Catholics, most of his subjects felt that the nationalist and protestant ideals of their proud Elizabethan past were being betrayed. This feeling intensified after the Thirty Years' War broke out on the continent, and above all when in 1620 James's daughter Elizabeth and her husband the Elector Palatine became refugees, their principality occupied by Spanish troops.

These humiliations and the growing disreputability of the king's service were driving an ominous new division through the political nation, a division between Court and Country. The terms came into contemporary usage in just this period. The 'Court interest' included not only what we should call courtiers but all who served the king in the central government and administration, all who wrung sinecures and other lucrative grants from his bounty, and by extension the many gentry in the counties who looked to his ministers and favourites as patrons. The Country by contrast embraced all those gentry who were free of dependence on the Court and were coming to regard it as a swollen and vicious parasite. The Court-Country cleavage showed clearly in the Addled Parliament of 1614, whose stormy sittings demonstrated on the one hand that James's government had quite lost the Tudor arts of managing parliament, and on the other that the Commons had not yet thrown up leaders of their own who could temper the tactics of opposition with responsible statesmanship.

This was a time too when the claims of the royal prerogative were increasingly questioned by the common lawyers, Coke chief among them. James's dismissal of Coke from the Chief Justiceship of the King's Bench in 1616 was a sad landmark, to be followed by further threats to the independence of the judiciary. To make matters worse, the prosperity of James's earlier years had by then collapsed, and the main cause was his own ill-judged decision to transfer the trading rights of the Merchant Adventurers, who controlled cloth exports to the Low Countries, to a mushroom syndicate headed by Alderman Cockayne. The crown's prerogative powers over the affairs of merchants were brought into still further disrepute by the multiplication of monopolies, and once again Buckingham and his protégés were the chief profiteers.

After a long lapse in parliamentary activity, the period from 1621 to 1629—our third stage—was one of frequent parliaments and mounting constitutional conflict. It began against a background of deepening economic depression. After a brief recovery from the Cockayne fiasco the cloth trade began to slump again even more disastrously, and a series of wretched harvests, coinciding with widespread unemployment, brought hunger and misery to many parts of England. This time the government was not to blame, for the causes lay in our war-wracked continental markets, but the traditional palliatives that the privy council applied never took the measure of the chronic depression in our one major industry. Recovery set in by 1625, but it was never more than partial and precarious.

The parliament of 1621 however was troubled even more by political than by economic discontents. It revived the process of impeachment, which had lain disused since the Wars of the Roses, and employed it to bring down one of the king's greatest ministers, Francis Bacon, now Viscount St. Albans and Lord Chancellor. The charge was that he took bribes, but his real offences were his association with Buckingham and his championship of the royal prerogative. More impeachments were to follow, and parliament was launched on its long struggle to render the king's ministers accountable to itself. In the same year the Commons dared to challenge the king on the hitherto sacred ground of foreign policy. Their clamour for war with Spain was foolish, yet three years later Buckingham joined the warmongers, and within two years more he had England at war with France as well as Spain. The results were a scale of expenditure that made the government desperate for supplies, and a series of military and naval disgraces that bred a bitter sense of national humiliation and a crescendo of fury against the favourite.

Charles I's accession in 1625 made little immediate difference, for the old king's grip had been slackening for some time and the new one was even more completely under Buckingham's sway. But in the parliament of that year the Commons abused their power of the purse by seeking to grant the customs duties of tonnage and poundage for one year only, and their successors of 1626 refused supplies for the war altogether until their grievances were redressed. They regarded Buckingham as 'the grievance of grievances', and only another dissolution prevented them from impeaching him. Charles then appealed directly to the nation for a free gift, and when that failed in face of the gentry's solid resistance he imposed a huge forced loan. Many gentlemen refused to pay and went to gaol, and some of them raised an important test case as to the crown's right to imprison them for reasons of state without trial. The judges found for the king, but the next parliament (1628) took up the cause of the subject's liberty most vigorously. The outcome was the Petition of Right, whereby Charles was forced to acknowledge that he could neither raise taxes, gifts nor loans without parliament's consent, nor imprison his subjects without declaring the cause and entitling them to a trial at law. Soon after this victory, the nation celebrated another deliverance: Buckingham was assassinated.

Yet early in 1629 the Commons threw off the statesmanlike restraint that had secured the Petition of Right and flew at the so-called Arminian divines who enjoyed Charles I's special patronage. These high churchmen, of whom William Laud was emerging as the leader, were obnoxious to ordinary protestant Englishmen, whether Puritans or not, on several grounds: their reintroduction of altars, vestments and liturgical practices that seemed to hark back to popery; their reaction—similarly suspect—against Calvinist theology; their high clerical pretensions, especially their claim that the office and authority of bishop were *jure divino*, ordained by the law of God; their preaching that it was sin to raise the least question of the king's authority; and their efforts to recover for the church some of the wealth of which it had been plundered since the reformation. The last parliamentary session before 1640 ended violently, with the Speaker held down weeping in his chair while the Commons acclaimed wild resolutions that anyone who promoted popery and Arminianism, or advised the levying of tonnage and poundage without parliament's consent, 'shall be reputed a capital enemy to this kingdom and commonwealth'. This suggestion that there were treasons against the state distinct from treasons against the king momentarily opened a glimpse into a terrifying future in which king, Lords and Commons, the three pillars of England's much-vaunted 'mixed monarchy', might fall irreparably apart.

Yet a long calm descended upon the country during the last phase before the Great Rebellion. These eleven years without a parliament have sometimes been called a tyranny, but they were not that. The crown assumed no new despotic powers; the counties went on as before under the rule of their leading families and the law took its customary course. Nor were they really years of personal rule by Charles I, for he quite lacked the zest and energy for such a rôle.

The true centre of national government reverted to the privy council, now no longer eclipsed by one imperious favourite but an arena once more for contending factions. Lord Treasurer Weston achieved a certain ascendancy in the early sixteen-thirties, Archbishop Laud in the later. The man of most formidable stature in the king's service, Thomas, Viscount Wentworth, was kept far from the hub of affairs, first in the Council of the North and then in Ireland, and was not admitted to Charles's full trust until 1639. Charles I's councillors were not an imposing lot, but their government was not notably inefficient or corrupt by the lowish standards of the time, and it did renounce some of the worst abuses of the Buckingham period.

Why then did this government become so hated that the political nation would finally accept its direction no longer? Some textbooks account for it too simply in terms of 'illegal' taxation and Puritan opposition to Archbishop Laud. The issues were really wider. Obviously, the financial expedients whereby the crown avoided recourse to parliament were disliked in themselves. Distraint of knighthood, the doubled revenues wrung from wardship, the new monopolies under the guise of corporations, the 'compositions' exacted for encroaching on long-forgotten royal forests or contravening obsolescent statutes against depopulation or building in the suburbs of London—all these smelt of legal chicanery and often bore harshly upon individuals. Ship money was hated more because it was a land tax in disguise and because it threatened to obviate the necessity for parliaments indefinitely.

Yet England remained one of the most lightly taxed countries in Europe, and Englishmen cared not only about what they had to pay but what they were paying for. More than half Charles's revenue went to sustain his court and courtiers, and the alienation between Court and Country was growing ever deeper. The court was no longer the splendid show-case through which Elizabeth had wooed her public, no longer the natural focus of the whole world of quality, no longer the proper centre to which honourable ambition and talent gravitated in the hope of a career of public service. To most of the gentry it seemed a côterie apart, alien to their aspirations and offensive to their prejudices. There were too many papists in high places, not only in the entourage of Queen Henrietta Maria but even in the privy council itself. Neither Charles nor Laud ever wavered in his Anglican loyalties, but the association between popery and Arminianism came naturally to the average protestant Englishman. Foreign policy seemed to bear it out, for the war with Spain was quickly wound up and through most of the 'thirties Charles reverted to the pro-Spanish alignment of his father's time. It went hard that England should aid the Spaniards in their renewed war against the Dutch Republic, where many an Englishman had shed his blood for the protestant cause.

The religion of Laud and the Arminians displayed itself more and more as a court religion. The king upheld the divine right of bishops; the bishops inflated the hitherto accepted divine right of kings into a doctrine of virtual absolutism. The prominent presence of the three highest prelates—the Archbishops of Canterbury and York and the Bishop of London—in the privy council went against a long tradition, and was much disliked. The courts of Star Chamber and High Commission were used more conspicuously to enforce a censorship and repress critics of the régime in church and state; the savage sentences on Prynne, Bastwick, Burton and Lilburne rebounded eventually upon those who inflicted them.

The most general grievance of all came to be that what contemporaries called the fundamental laws, and we would call the constitution, were being deliberately subverted; that parliament was suppressed so that government could pursue policies in church and state that were abhorrent to most of the nation. Resistance, especially to the payment of ship money, was already beginning when in 1638 rebellion broke out in Scotland against the imposition of a prayer book similar to England's. The king's government in Scotland rapidly collapsed, and Charles's attempt to restore it by English arms failed ignominiously. Too many of his English subjects had sympathy more with the Scots' cause than with his. After this military fiasco, in 1639 Charles at last called Wentworth home to be his chief minister and made him Earl of Strafford. On Strafford's advice he summoned the first parliament for eleven years, but this Short Parliament would do nothing for him unless he redressed a comprehensive list of grievances, and he dissolved it after only three weeks. Strafford advised him that he was now 'loose and absolved from all rules of government', and in the brief interval before the reckoning came England caught a whiff of real tyranny. But in the second 'Bishops' War' of 1640 the Scots marched first, drove the English militia back from the river Tyne in disorder, and forced Charles to conclude a humiliating truce. They were to remain in occupation of the northern counties, and England was to pay their keep.

III

Nothing could now save Charles, try as he would, from calling another parliament. The Long Parliament met on 3 November 1640, and within ten months it carried through the decisive victory of the Country over the Court. The Court element in the Commons was the smallest on record, and it was helpless against the serried ranks of opposition that John Pym marshalled so skilfully. Strafford and Laud were promptly impeached, and when Strafford's prosecutors failed to pin charges on him that the Lords would accept as treason, they hustled him to the scaffold with an arbitrary act of attainder. By that time Pym and his supporters were already tackling the abuses of the last decade with a momentous series of constitutional bills, and Charles, with two armies to be paid and no resources, was powerless to refuse them.

Yet these Country politicians were mostly conservative rather than revolutionary in spirit. They wanted to restore the equilibrium of the 'balanced polity' which they had inherited from the Tudors, and which Charles I had tilted—though not so far as they made out—in the direction of continental absolutism. All the famous statutes that they passed in 1641 claimed a basis in existing law and precedent, though neither their law nor their history was very sound. Taken together, these acts marked a considerable advance towards constitutional monarchy, yet they left the essential prerogatives of the crown intact, and a wiser king than Charles would have accepted them with a better grace. The Triennial Act provided that henceforth not more than three years should ever elapse without a session of parliament. Another act secured that the present parliament—it applied to no others—should not be dissolved without its own consent. Two more acts abolished the court of Star chamber, together with the prerogative jurisdiction of the Councils in the North and in the Marches, and the High Commission. The Tonnage and Poundage Act made all duties levied at the ports, new impositions as well as old customs, subject to parliamentary consent. Further statutes condemned ship money and the other financial expedients of the 'thirties, and closed the remaining loopholes for non-parliamentary taxation. Parliament thus assured its regular summons in the future, strengthened its power of the purse and established the clear supremacy of the common law, but so far it still left England with a monarch who could rule as well as reign.

There remained the question of religion, and on this the members were less united. It was probably only because the Lords rejected a bill to exclude the bishops from the upper House that the Commons debated a more radical one that would have abolished the whole ecclesiastical hierarchy 'root and branch'. Yet this Root and Branch Bill was dropped in the end, and the signs were that the moderate majority in both Houses would settle for some modifications of episcopal authority and of the prayer book rather than permit the abolition of either.

By the late summer of 1641, when parliament treated itself to its first recess, the fierce tensions of the past year were relaxing. The Scots had signed a treaty and withdrawn, and the English forces that had faced them were being disbanded. The measures already passed were as much as most moderate men wanted, and the country looked forward to a fresh start on the now tolerably secure basis of constitutional monarchy. Yet within a year England was plunged in civil war. Why?

The event which did most to precipitate the crisis was the appalling rebellion which broke out in Ulster in October and then spread rapidly through most of Ireland. The story of massacre and atrocity was heightened a hundredfold in the telling, and it magnified the bogy of popery into a huge spectre, menacing England herself. It sharpened acutely the opposition's distrust of Charles, for the Irish rebels falsely claimed his sanction for their seizure of protestant property. Charles himself gave too much ground for distrust by his absence in Scotland, whither he had gone in August in the hope of building up a party for himself among the Scottish nobles. The Irish terror necessitated the raising of a new army in England, yet if military power were put into the king's hands—and there was neither law nor precedent for putting it in anyone else's—could he be trusted to use it only against the Irish? This question enabled Pym to press for an answer to another that the parliament had so far left still open: the question of how to ensure that the king governed through ministers who commanded parliament's confidence, without encroaching on his hitherto undoubted right to choose his own servants. Pym now launched a frontal attack on that right. On 8 November he carried the Commons in a demand that the king should 'employ only such counsellors and ministers as should be approved by his parliament'—or else parliament would take the suppression of the Irish rebellion into its own hands. A fortnight later the Commons passed the Grand Remonstrance, but by a majority of only eleven. Nominally addressed to the king, it was really a manifesto to the nation of all that evil counsellors had done amiss in the past fifteen years and all that parliament intended by way of redress. In December and January Pym went further and bid for parliamentary control over the militia. It was the gravest encroachment on the royal prerogative that the Commons had yet dared.

Outside the walls of the parliament-house the atmosphere of crisis was growing thicker. The crowds that had clamoured for Strafford's head were out again in the London streets, rabbling the bishops on their way to the house of lords. Twelve of them protested that they dared no longer attend and that parliament's proceedings were void in their absence. Pym promptly impeached them. A few days later the annual elections to the Common Council of London swung decisively his way, and he found means soon after of securing the government of the City in the hands of his allies. Then in the first week of 1642 Charles committed his crowning blunder by going to the House of Commons in person to arrest Pym and four other leaders of the opposition. The City gave them refuge and called out its militia, and for a hectic week London wore the aspect of a great capital on the verge of revolution.

The immediate storm died down, and anxious men on both sides laboured to avert the threat of civil war. But the essential issues over which the war would be fought were already defined, and from now on the political nation was steadily driven towards one camp or the other. Should parliament wrest control over the militia from the crown? Should the king's choice of ministers and officers of state be subjected to parliamentary approval? Should parliament initiate a thorough reformation of the national church, and if so were episcopacy and the liturgy to be merely reformed or struck down root and branch? The radicals' demands on these points went far beyond the limited constitutional objectives of the acts that the parliament had passed so far. Unlike those acts, they could claim no basis in the ancient fundamental laws; no cloak of antiquarian respectability could be thrown over a programme that could now fairly be called revolutionary. As the issues changed, so did the alignment of parties. Between the Grand Remonstrance of November 1641 and the outbreak of war nine months later, the nation divided between Royalists and Parliamentarians, and the line of division was very different from that between Court and Country in 1640. Many of the old Country interest that had supported the legislation of 1641 were dismayed at the demands that Pym was now pressing and at his methods of enlisting support for them. Charles rallied them to his side with a series of skilful and conciliatory declarations which were largely the work of one of their own number, Edward Hyde, the future Earl of Clarendon. The old Court interest was equally split. Although many fought for the king, many others retreated into neutrality, and a sizable minority went over to the Parliamentarians.

Most Englishmen faced the threat of civil war with extreme reluctance, and the division between the two sides was never clear-cut or complete. Recent research has shown what a considerable proportion of the political nation remained neutral, or at least as neutral as it expediently could. There were of course fully committed men on both sides: 'old cavaliers' who regarded the parliament-dogs as mere rebels, and radicals who wanted a decisive transfer of executive as well as legislative power to parliament. Without them there would have been no Civil War. But the majority, even of those who engaged themselves on either side, did not see the issues in such black-and-white terms. Many Parliamentarians had no real wish either for further constitutional changes beyond those of 1641 or for the abolition of episcopacy; they were just uneasily persuaded that

Charles could not be trusted to honour what he had been forced to concede unless his hands were further tied. Many Royalists on the other hand approved the recent statutes and disliked popery and Arminianism no less than their more moderate opponents. Between these large moderate groups on either side there was no profound difference of principle; their choice mainly depended on whether they regarded the untrustworthiness of the king or the risks and stigma of rebellion as the greater evil. When allegiance was so often divided by a hair's breadth, and when it so often shifted from one side to the other or hung uneasily poised between the two, we should be very wary of entertaining any simple or single explanation of the alignment of parties on the eve of civil war.

The line of division between Royalists and Parliamentarians, though different from that between Court and Country in the recent past, still ran right through the ruling class of Stuart England. Every order of society, every kind of occupation, was represented in considerable numbers on both sides. The motives that inclined men one way or the other were varied. Loyalty to the king might stem from simple sentiment or from a professional career in the royal service, and either way it was commonly reinforced by affection for the Anglican church order and liturgy, attachment to the old fundamental laws of the land, and a dread lest all this whipping up of popular support and arming of the people against their betters should subvert the whole social order that held the ranks and degrees of men in their due places. There was a note of fear in the social contempt which the cavaliers so often professed towards their adversaries. Motivation on the parliamentary side probably ranged still more widely. Radicals like Henry Parker, the pamphleteer, believed that sovereignty derived from the people and that the people's representatives should be the final arbiters in a national crisis like that of 1642—provided that the nobles and gentry in parliament maintained the exclusive right to speak for the people. There were probably some on the fringes of the political nation who questioned even this proviso, though their voices would not be heard much just yet. More general was a negative determination to put it out of the power of 'evil counsellors' at court to do the country further harm. Puritans naturally backed parliament's demand for a thorough reformation of religion, and many (like Richard Baxter) whose religious aims were not very radical were swayed by their moral judgment upon the king's party. Others were moved more by wrongs suffered at the hands of the king's agents during the years of arbitrary rule, and others again by frustration in their business enterprises through the crown's abuse of economic regulation. In some counties, moreover, the split ran much along the lines of purely local feuds and factions.

There was a rough geographical division between the two sides. East Anglia, the south-east and south were predominantly Parliamentarian, while the king's cause was strongest in the south-west, in Wales and the border-counties and in the far north. Not surprisingly, Puritanism was strong in most of the former areas and religious conservatism (whether Anglican or Roman Catholic) in the latter. The Parliamentarian regions were also richer, more populous, generally more advanced both in agriculture and industry, the Royalist ones sparser, poorer and more backward. There are many difficulties however in the way of accepting the Marxist thesis that this line of cleavage implied a kind of class antagonism between a 'bourgeois' type of landowner on the one side and a 'feudal' type on the other. Yet it does look as though impoverished gentility was temperamentally more inclined to Royalism than to its opposite, and this despite Professor Trevor-Roper's theory that the core of radical opposition lay in the declining gentry of the backwoods. The remoter Royalist regions were thick with small, struggling gentlemen who were mostly as loyal as their greater neighbours, and we know that in some divided counties such as Yorkshire a higher proportion of Royalist than of Parliamentarian gentry were in financial straits. The geographical division however was far from clear-cut, for right down the centre of England from Yorkshire and Lancashire to Somerset and Wiltshire ran a chain of divided or disputed counties, and no shire in England was without some supporters of each side.

Turning to the main social groups, many more peers fought for the king than against him, though the Parliamentarian minority was quite formidable. The landed gentry however played much the most important part in both the fighting and the politics of the Civil War years and they were much more evenly divided. It is likely that over England as a whole rather more of the leading county families just below the peerage were for the king, though not by any means in every county. About the lesser gentry historians are still busy finding out, for the regional variation was very great. Professor Supple warns us in a later chapter against generalizing glibly about the merchants, but for all the many important exceptions the majority were for the parliament. Over large areas of England the towns stood out in opposition to a predominantly Royalist countryside, as did the rural clothing areas in the West Riding, in Lancashire and elsewhere. Several contemporaries remarked how much support the parliament got from 'the middling sort'—yeomen, substantial tenant farmers, traders and clothiers in a modest way of business, solid independent craftsmen and the like. This is broadly true, though the middling sort then did not mean the same as what we understand by the middle classes. Below this level of society it is not safe to generalize, for the degree of involvement varied so much, and so does the surviving evidence.

Perhaps historians concentrate too much on the line-up of parties at the outbreak of war. It had already changed greatly since Court and Country first faced each other in the Long Parliament, and it would change again as the revolution became more radical in the later 'forties. The ranks would re-align and further sub-divide, for the Civil War engendered more conflicts than it resolved.

As late as February 1642 there seemed nothing inevitable about the drift into civil war. Pym's hold on the parliament could still be precarious; the king's declarations sounded plausible and his concessions tempting. Charles actually assented to an act excluding bishops from the House of Lords. He offered high office to former opponents, even to Pym himself. He was even prepared to treat, too late, over the militia and the objectionable ceremonies in Anglican worship. The trouble was that his public declarations spoke with one voice and his actions with another. Space forbids a re-telling of the intrigues and blunders that undermined confidence in him, but they played into Pym's hands. When parliament passed the Militia Ordinance in March and claimed for it the full force of law despite the refusal of the royal assent, the hopes of a peaceful settlement dwindled fast. Charles withdrew to York, and when he summoned the loyal peers and M.P.s to his side he left the radical men firmly in command at Westminster. Their demands inevitably grew more uncompromising. Both sides raised forces during the summer, and on 22 August Charles gave the formal signal for war by raising his standard at Nottingham.

We cannot follow the course of the fighting, but the changing fortunes of battle gave rise to two developments which greatly affected the political and religious outcome. The first happened when parliament, brought near to defeat in the summer of 1643, allied with the Scots. The Solemn League and Covenant between the two nations gave Scotland a voice in the eventual settlement and pledged England to establish a Presbyterian national church. But although Scottish arms helped to win the great battle of Marston Moor in July 1644, this was not the decisive victory that it should have been. Parliament's generals, the Earls of Essex and Manchester, did not want to fight the war to a finish. They feared that the consequences would go far beyond their original war aims, vague as those were, and they were anxious for a negotiated peace. Death had removed Pym from his struggle to prevent the parliament from splitting between a war party and a peace party, and the split opened wide when Oliver Cromwell charged Manchester, his own general, before the House of Commons for his 'backwardness to all action'. It was not a personal vendetta, for as soon as the charge was substantiated Cromwell and his allies dropped it in favour of more positive measures: the resignation of all peers and M.P.s from their military commands and the forging of an instrument of total victory in the New Model Army.

The New Model, with Sir Thomas Fairfax as Lord General and Cromwell at the head of the cavalry, took the field in 1645. It won the decisive battle of Naseby in June and brought the whole war to an end a year later, but its impact on the course of the revolution had only just begun. Charles surrendered to the Scots, knowing how disquieted they were at the radical Independent temper of the New Model Army. Indeed they were inclined to help him back to his throne if he would only take the Covenant and guarantee a Presbyterian settlement of religion in England as well as Scotland. This he would not do; nor would he accept the severe terms offered to him by the English parliament. The Scots handed him over to the parliament's custody, but he was not too dismayed. He had already begun a long game of temporizing and intrigue, and he reckoned to exploit the divisions among his enemies until either they lowered their conditions or he succeeded in raising military assistance abroad.

The parliament was indeed divided, and the broad cleavage between conservative and radical factions extended, as Mr. Pennington later describes, to the county committees which had managed the war effort at the local level. One set of issues was political, and arose from the problems of settling the kingdom in face of the king's refusal of parliament's terms. The other great issue was religion, and I touch in a later chapter on the contest between monolithic Presbyterianism and the Independents' plea for liberty of conscience. Contemporaries labelled the two main parliamentary groupings 'Presbyterian' and 'Independent', whether the matter of debate was political or religious, and in spite of the fact that in these two quite different contexts the line of division was by no means the same: political conservatives were not necessarily Presbyterians by religious conviction, nor were all the radical men religious Independents. What broadly characterized the 'political' Presbyterians was a desire to restore the king as soon as possible, a profound distrust of the New Model's intentions, acute sensitivity to any threat against the established hierarchy of rank and degree (such as they sensed in the army and in the Puritan sects), and reluctance to consider any political changes beyond what were necessary to secure the interests of their own kind. The Independents covered a wider political spectrum, ranging from moderates, who differed from the Presbyterians more in tactics than in principles, to genuine radicals, the nucleus of a republican party. They opposed any sell-out to the king; they were readier to consider constitutional and legal reforms whose benefits would extend beyond the traditional ruling class; they looked to the army as allies, being generally outvoted in parliament; and if they were not tolerationists by conviction (as many were) they were impelled that way by their dependence on the army.

The Presbyterians wanted to disband the army as soon as possible, and in the war-weary, over-taxed, economically depressed England of 1647 they naturally had much support in this aim. But they pursued it with such a shabby disregard for the soldiers' rights, including their arrears of pay, and put such blatant slights upon the men who had won their battles, that the regiments spontaneously elected 'Agitators' from the rank and file to represent their grievances. By one provocation after another the Presbyterians drove the army into open revolt. It broke out in June when the regiments marched in defiance of parliament's orders to a general rendezvous at Newmarket. Cornet Joyce carried the king off to join them there, and thither fled Cromwell, threatened now by the Presbyterians with impeachment. Officers and soldiers covenanted together not to disband until their grievances—and not theirs only but the people's—were redressed. They were talking now of much larger matters than their arrears of pay. They demanded that parliament should expel their detractors, fix a date for its own dissolution, reform its whole constitution by a rational redistribution of seats, and provide for future elections at short and regular intervals. The army, in fact, was claiming to speak for the people of England. In order to give it a single voice and to keep the Agitators within bounds, its commanders established a General Council of the Army on which each regiment was represented by two officers and two soldiers, elected by their fellows.

The Presbyterian politicians at first showed some fight, and then, when they began to yield to the army's intimidation, a mob of Londoners invaded the House of Commons and forced it to call the king back to his capital. Fairfax marched his troops in and cowed both parliament and City. But force would not in itself settle the kingdom's problems, and the generals were already seeking another solution by negotiating with Charles themselves. The pacemaker in this as in most other political moves by the army was Cromwell's very gifted son-in-law, Commissary-General Ireton. His 'Heads of the Proposals' for a conditional reinstatement of the king were in most ways more statesmanlike than the parliament's terms—more concerned with positive political reforms, more tolerant in religion, more lenient to the beaten Royalists and less of an affront to traditional regal authority. But there were three obstacles to their acceptance. The first was Charles himself, who temporized over them as he had over parliament's offers, vainly confident that time or force would bring them both lower. Then there was the question of how to make parliament accept them, even if Charles did. Finally, a growing section of the army was rebelling against the whole negotiation. The Leveller movement had been taking shape in London since the previous year, and by the autumn of 1647 it had formulated a programme for a popular commonwealth that had no place in it for either king or lords. The Levellers were working on the army through its Agitators, and in September five regiments elected new Agitators of a still more radical colour who became the spearhead of an effort to enlist the entire soldiery, if necessary in defiance of their officers, in support of a new political deal based on the suffrages of all the free people of England. Faced with the implacable hostility of the parliament and of the ruling class it represented, the Levellers were bidding for control of the army in order to forge it into an instrument of revolutionary action. The crucial confrontation between the army commanders and the Leveller-indoctrinated Agitators took place in the famous Putney Debates, which figure so largely in Dr. Manning's chapter.

The whole situation was more tangled and uncertain than at any time since the first outbreak of war. Charles however choose to cut through it with a sword. In November 1647, a few days after the debates at Putney, he fled from the army's custody to Carisbrooke in the Isle of Wight. There, even if he did not win the Governor to his side as he had hoped, he managed to negotiate with certain commissioners from Scotland without the army chiefs breathing down his neck. A new party had taken over from the strict Covenanters in Scotland, a party which was headed by Charles's old councillor the Duke of Hamilton and was ready to fight for his restoration without forcing him or his subjects to take the Covenant against their wills. On 26 December Charles signed a fatal Engagement with Hamilton's commissioners, they undertaking to send an army to his aid, he to call the cavaliers to arms once more.

The secret could not be kept for long. The army closed its ranks; generals and Agitators joined in vowing to bring 'Charles Stuart, that man of blood' to account for his crimes. The parliament was more divided, but in January it voted to treat with him no further. The second Civil War began in the spring of 1648 with a series of Royalist risings, the greatest being the one in Kent which Professor

Everitt discusses later. Their gallantry was thrown to waste because the Scots failed to march soon enough to support them. They were all either defeated or contained by the time in August that Cromwell fell upon the Scots at Preston and annihilated them in a three-days' running fight. The war was then virtually over, and Charles was a ruined gambler.

Yet even now it seemed that his ruin might not be total. Moderate men had seen in this last war a choice of evils—a choice between a restoration carried by Scottish arms or the final triumph of the army and its Independent allies. The one would bring an unbridled Royalist reaction; the other starkly threatened monarchy itself. And with monarchy the whole system of gentry power and social subordination stood in danger, for even if the Levellers were checked, the displacement of the ruling county families by lesser men, already widely apparent, would be bound to go further. So the Presbyterian politicians reopened negotiations with Charles and desperately sought agreement with him all through the late autumn. It was more than the army could stand. Ireton really took charge now, for Fairfax was miserably torn and Cromwell took refuge from decision in the siege of Royalist Pontefract. The army secured the king once more, marched into London early in December and purged the parliament by forcibly excluding the Presbyterian majority. Cromwell arrived on the scene at last; his long spell of perplexed self-communing had characteristically given way to a mood of fierce resolution. The Independent remnant of the House of Commons charged the king with waging war upon the people of England and erected a High Court of Justice consisting of its own more radical members and a large stiffening of army officers. Charles refused to plead before this revolutionary tribunal, but its purpose was inexorable. His head fell on a scaffold before Whitehall Palace on 30 January, 1649.

The Rump of the Long Parliament now became the supreme authority in a commonwealth without either king or House of Lords. Thus the conflict between Presbyterians and Independents was resolved by force, but there still remained the latent conflict between the Independents (of both Army and Rump) and the Levellers. It did not remain latent for long. The Levellers had been deluded into hoping that the army grandees would sponsor at least a modified version of their plan for a popular commonwealth based on an Agreement of the People. The Council of Officers debated it, diluted it, presented it to the Rump and allowed it to be quietly shelved. Instead of representative government broad-based on the people's suffrages, the Levellers confronted an oligarchy of calculating politicians, many of them elected more than eight years ago and all sustained by the sharp swords of the grandees. Once more they set in motion their machinery of pamphlets, petitions and mass demonstrations, and this time they raised quite serious mutinies in the army. But their hold on the soldiery could not really challenge that of Fairfax and Cromwell, and after the crushing of the mutinies their movement lost cohesion and declined.

To do the army leaders justice, the Rump was not the kind of government they really wanted, but they knew how precariously the young Commonwealth stood and how fatal a genuine appeal to the people would have been after the fearful shock of the king's execution. They faced an immediate threat from Ireland, where Cromwell conducted a ruthless campaign. Within a year a no less serious danger from Scotland called him home, for the young Charles II swallowed his pride and put himself and his cause into the hands of the Scottish Covenanters. Cromwell now took Fairfax's place as Lord General, for Fairfax had scruples about attacking former allies with whom he had sworn the Solemn League and Covenant, and he resigned. But England had either to invade or be invaded. Cromwell never found a tougher enemy than his old comrade-in-arms David Leslie, or saved himself more spectacularly from defeat than in his superb victory at Dunbar on 3 September, 1650. But the young king still had friends and arms to call upon in Scotland, and next summer he staked them all upon a southward march into England. It ended at Worcester, a year to the day after Dunbar—for Cromwell the 'crowning mercy', for the Royalists the last appearance on an English battlefield.

After three hard seasons of campaigning, Cromwell and the army now came back into politics. Their dissatisfaction with their parliamentary masters grew steadily stronger. The Rump would not undertake to dissolve itself before November 1654; it temporized endlessly over the settlement of religion and the reform of the law;

it kept old sores open by confiscating hundreds of minor Royalist estates; it offended Cromwell's ideal of a united 'protestant interest' by making war on the Dutch. The army's accusations of general corruption were much exaggerated, but its basic grievance was that these worldly-minded politicians had no real care for 'the interest of the people of God' and were sticking like leeches to their positions of power and profit. The final crisis came in April 1653 when the Rump tried to rush through a bill whereby the sitting members would retain their places and elections would be held only to the vacant seats. Cromwell's answer was that famous file of musketeers which cleared the chamber and locked its doors.

What happened next can only be understood in the light of the mounting religious enthusiasm in the army that I touch on in a later chapter. A vociferous minority, headed by Major-General Harrison, were convinced that the millennium was at hand, when Antichrist was to be overthrown and 'the saints shall take the kingdom and possess it'. Cromwell's vision was less crude than Harrison's, but he too thought he glimpsed 'the day of the power of Christ'. He could not summon an elected parliament anyway; not only had he no legal right, but having made enemies in turn of the Royalist, the Presbyterian and now most of the Independent politicians, he could expect only hostility and confusion from such a body. So he and the Council of Officers decided on a nominated assembly as the new supreme authority, and they chose and summoned 139 'men fearing God, and of approved integrity' to represent England (by counties), Wales, Scotland and Ireland. Unfortunately the officers were not at one in what they expected of this assembly. Cromwell and his more realistic colleagues envisaged a temporary government which was to educate the nation in the blessings of a commonwealth until it could once more safely choose its own governors, and they nominated mostly men of some substance and experience. Harrison and the fanatics, by contrast, intended a rule of the saints in preparation for the imminent reign of Christ as king, and they named many obscure sectarian zealots. No wonder Barebone's Parliament, as it came to be called, tended to split between a moderate majority and a firebrand minority. The latter attempted to abrogate the whole common law in favour of a simple written code; they aimed to abolish not only tithes but lay patronage over parish livings and indeed any kind of established ministry in the church. To Cromwell they seemed to be threatening not only religion but property too, and he was thoroughly relieved when in December, after five months' sitting, the moderate majority walked out in disgust and resigned their authority back into his hands.

There was nothing for it now but to take up the burden himself, for as he said 'we were running headlong into confusion and disorder.' He accepted a written constitution, the Instrument of Government, from the hands of a small group of officers headed by Major-General Lambert, and on 16 December, 1653 he was installed as Lord Protector. Government now returned to a more traditional pattern, for Protector, council of state and parliament as defined by the Instrument, were modified versions of monarch, privy council and parliament as envisaged by the reformers of the 'forties. Executive and legislative powers were to be separated, and the old ideal of a 'balanced polity' was reaffirmed. The Protector had to obtain the council's consent in all significant decisions of policy, and his power of veto over bills passed by parliament, provided they did not contravene the Instrument itself, was limited to twenty days. Parliaments were to be elected at least every three years under a moderate property franchise, and their seats were completely reapportioned so that the majority went to the counties and only the larger towns got separate representation.

Cromwell and the council were given emergency powers of legislation until the first new parliament met, and they used it to tackle the thorny problem of religious settlement. They rejected the Leveller and sectarian claim that religion should be wholly removed from the civil magistrate's authority. They provided for a parochial ministry, to be approved by a mixed commission of 'Triers' and supported by tithes until a less objectionable form of contribution could be devised. But they imposed no set order of worship, no formal confession of faith and no compulsory ecclesiastical discipline, while the Instrument itself guaranteed the freedom of the peaceable sects to associate and worship in their own way.

The Protectorate was not a dictatorship, either in intent or even for the most part in practice. Yet Cromwell's sincere desire for 'a government by consent' was frustrated by two harsh facts. Firstly, the constitution had been framed by a junto of officers and depended on the army to sustain it. Secondly, the parliamentary cause had undergone such fragmentation since 1642 that any basis for unity was desperately hard to find. Faced with Royalists, Presbyterians, Rumpers, Levellers, Commonwealthsmen opposed to the rule of any single person and millenarians dedicated to a dictatorship of the saints, 'where,' cried Cromwell, 'shall we find that consent?' Yet 'healing and settling' was the constant theme of his speeches. He strove to reconcile the traditional political nation to a government that would set a bulwark against any further threat of social revolution and preserve 'the ranks and orders of men, whereby England hath been known for hundreds of years: a nobleman, a gentleman, a yeoman. That,' he said, 'is a good interest of the nation, and a great one.'[6]

It was uphill work, and like the Stuarts before him he found the limits of his success registered in his relations both with parliament and with the county communities. Two parliaments met under his Protectorate, and in each of them only arbitrary measures prevented the republican politicians who had managed the Rump from leading the majority of moderate, uncommitted members in dangerous attacks upon his personal authority and upon the whole constitution under which he ruled. As for the gentry in the counties, it would be a distortion to picture them seething continuously with discontent, for the signs are that their old ties of neighbourhood were being steadily re-knit. Yet they shared a common dislike for a 'sword government', and most of the older ruling families remained unreconciled either to their regicide masters or to the newer and lesser men who had in so many cases supplanted them in county office. Cromwell's most drastic measure to compel their co-operation was his division of England into eleven districts, each under a major-general. This followed the abortive Royalist risings of 1655, and its prime object was to provide military security against further conspiracy. But as Professor Roots points out in the next chapter, the powers of surveillance over local government which Cromwell

[6] *Writings and Speeches of Oliver Cromwell*, ed. W. C. Abbott (Cambridge, Mass., 1937–47), iii. 435.

gave to the major-generals were a measure of his failure to gain the gentry's collaboration, and nothing did his reputation more harm than his commissioning of upstart soldiers to tell the 'natural' rulers of the county communities how to go about their business. Yet it should be remembered that when parliament pronounced against the major-generals' régime, less than eighteen months after its inception, Cromwell acquiesced in its sentence.

Cromwell certainly owed some of his difficulties to his innocence of the arts of parliamentary management and to his riding too roughly over the susceptibilities of local interests. But there was more to it than mere tactics. Certain policies which he thought it his mission to uphold were so contrary to the prejudices of most of the nobility and gentry that no amount of politicking would have won their general acceptance in his time. Not even purged parliaments or well-winnowed benches of justices would go all the way with him on liberty of conscience—still less on his ideal of a 'reformation of manners' (and here we may sympathize with them). Nor would most of them support him far in humanizing the criminal law, or promoting measures of social justice, or encouraging schemes for popular education. It is a mistake to regard the Protectorate as simply a phase of conservative reaction.

Moreover Cromwell did not wholly fail in his efforts at reconciliation. Very many of the gentry came to accept his rule as preferable to any likely alternative, so long as the Royalist cause lay in ruins. Men of conservative and even Royalist backgrounds like Lord Broghill, Charles Howard, George Monck and Sir Charles Wolseley rose high in his service. The trouble was that, as their influence rose and challenged that of the army officers and Puritan radicals, a new division began to appear. It opened wide during parliament's debates on the major-generals, and again when parliament invited Cromwell to assume the crown—a move inspired by these conservative Cromwellians, and sharply and successfully opposed by the officers. When Cromwell died in September 1658 he left his task of reunifying the nation in a sadly unfinished state. Yet paradoxically the short-lived rule of his son Richard probably enjoyed a broader basis of gentry support than any other government in the last ten years or more.

It was not a Royalist reaction that overthrew Richard's Protectorate and opened the way to the collapse of the revolution but a combination of radical groups who felt that the progressive return to more traditional ways was betraying the 'Good Old Cause' for which they had fought. The republican politicians of the Rump directed a skilful propaganda at the Commonwealthsmen in the army and the more fanatical sects. The chief officers lost their nerve and deserted Richard's sinking ship, and when they forced him to dissolve his parliament in April 1659 their unruly subordinates soon compelled them to restore the Rump to the supreme authority it had enjoyed down to 1653. But both Rump and army were politically bankrupt. They quarrelled again with each other as they had quarrelled before, and from October onwards all was in confusion. Behind the futile posturings of these last legatees of the great parliamentary cause that Pym had led in 1642, England drifted into anarchy and the Great Rebellion collapsed from within. Monarchy returned to fill a vacuum; it had rapidly become the only conceivable basis on which to re-establish the rule of law. The cool midwifery of General Monck assisted its rebirth, and a huge wave of popular acclaim for King Charles II threatened to engulf everything both good and bad that the Good Old Cause had stood for. In their haste to put the clock back, few men probably realized how deeply the experience of the past twenty years would remain etched upon the political, social and intellectual life of the nation. Fewer still would have guessed how soon—a mere twenty-eight years—another revolution would vindicate much of what Pym had striven for; or that more than six times that span would elapse before parliament began seriously to reform its own constitution or enlarge the political nation.

The Central Government and the Local Community

IVAN ROOTS

For all its show of majesty the most significant thing about the government of Elizabeth I was its underlying weakness. This was something shared by all sixteenth- and seventeenth-century governments whether they were royal, parliamentarian or protectoral.

They were hampered first of all by disputable constitutional restraints. Both the claims of ancient prerogative under Charles I and the plea of necessity under Cromwell were met by defences of the liberties and property of the subject. The law, traditionally one of the main instruments of government, now seemed to come increasingly into conflict with it. If the judges, Bacon's 'lions under the throne', were fairly domesticated beasts, they were also a bit unpredictable, and one or two, like Sir Edward Coke, even proved uncommandable. Appeals to ambiguous precedents or to conveniently undefined fundamental laws were reinforced by the activities of some members of parliament who took to asserting the interests, as they saw them, of the privileged minorities they represented against the demands of central authority.

The executive did not win all the arguments. Financial difficulties played a big part here. Prices had risen and expenditure, not all of it well-directed, was rising faster than administrations could expand recognized sources of revenue, and would-be strong government, especially an active foreign policy like that of Buckingham in the sixteen-twenties or Cromwell's thirty years later, is never cheap. There were limits to how much money could be raised and in what ways. There was always the risk of paying for increased resources by an unwelcome reduction in the freedom of action of the ruler. Penury made the sinews of government creak.

All this is obvious enough. A less often recognized inhibition was sheer lack of information—of vital statistics. Governments never knew how many people they ruled nor how their subjects and their wealth were distributed. They could not even be sure if the population was rising or falling. So they had to muddle through, taking by guess-work decisions which today would call for immense preliminary investigation. Because they had become by practice adept at living from hand to mouth they seem more systematic than they actually were. It was tidy-minded historians, not seventeenth-century statesmen, who invented the mercantile system. This assumption that governments were consistently concerned to use the power of the state to maximize national wealth has not been very helpful in explaining the harsh economic realities of the Stuart era. Social policies by governments such as that of Charles I during the so-called 'personal rule' (1629–40) which suggest some kind of premature welfare policy were, in fact, ways of keeping the people quiet when the state lacked, as it mostly did, the means to put down popular outbreaks.

This is made clear in a letter from the privy council to Rutland J.P.s in 1631, a year of slump. It had learned through a local minister —governments, in the absence of anything like a local bureaucracy, had to rely upon the busybody, the paid informer or someone with an interest—that a shoemaker of Uppingham was stirring up insurrection, saying that

> 'the poor men of Oakham have sent to us poor men of Uppingham, and if you poor men of Liddington will join with us, we will rise, and the poor of Oakham say they can have all the armour of the country in their power within half an hour, and (in faith, saith he) we will rifle the churls.'

The council was reluctant to put too much weight on 'the ejaculations of mean and contemptible persons', yet 'because it sorts well with the care and providence of a state to prevent all occasions which ill-affected persons may otherwise lay hold of under pretence and colour of the necessity of the time', they decided to order the deputy-lieutenants and the J.P.s to take good care of the county magazine and, 'which is indeed the most considerable and the best means to prevent all disorders in this kind', to see that local markets were well supplied with cheap corn. They were also to enforce the poor laws, making sure 'the richer sort' met their obligations to set the poor on work.[1]

The council always expected speedy reports from local officials of what they were doing. But the authorities they leaned upon were all too often unreliable agents of royal policy. An Essex farmer, found guilty by Star Chamber of 'enhancing the price . . . by keeping in his corn in this time of scarcity . . . an offence as well against the common law as against some statutes', blandly told the court that that local justices had neglected royal orders to inspect his barns.[2] It was not an isolated instance. There was plenty of law against this sort of offence, but what was lacking was the will of the justices to enforce it. They could not always see the point of actions designed to check the 'greedy cormorants' who played the market in food-supply. Many, of course, were agricultural producers themselves, but equally some had a sincere contrary point of view embedded in what seemed at least to themselves a genuine social concern. Thus Sir John Oglander, Governor of the Isle of Wight, was forced once or twice by the high price of corn to forbid export to the mainland. But he advised 'all men' to be very chary of doing this because in stopping 'the country' from selling its grain at the best rates, income would be lost that could have been used to set the poor on work. So 'whereas you think to help, you may undo the poor.' This in itself would encourage disorders among 'the meaner sort of people, who are always apt to rebel and mutiny'. Yet obviously in a dearth something must be done to quieten them. Oglander's solution was to use his personality—he was a smug man. He records that he had had 300 poor men with him 'in a morning' and had 'pacified them well', offering the kind words that in such a time could do more than harsh

---

[1] Privy Council Register, vi. f. 345, printed in E. M. Leonard, *The Early History of English Poor Relief* (1900), pp. 338–9.
[2] *Reports of Cases in the Courts of Star Chamber and High Commission*, ed. S. R. Gardiner (Camden Soc., n.s. xxxix, 1886), p. 44.

deeds. When things had settled, however, he had proceeded sternly against the ringleaders.[3]

What Oglander was claiming was that men on the spot knew better than those framing general policy away in London. He may have been right. His notebooks also give an insistent indication of another major inhibition on thorough, uniform government at this time: 'localism'. Localism meant a priority given to the apparent needs of a community smaller and more intimate than the state or nation. It was the expression of stubborn local patriotism backed by living traditions of provincial independence and was to be found throughout the realm. In 1632 Sir David Foulis rallied his 'country-men' of Yorkshire by reminding them that they had been reckoned stout fellows ready to stand up for the liberties of 'the worthiest of all other shires in the kingdom'. Formerly others had depended upon them and would try to copy their actions. But now it seemed they had degenerated. Only in James Mauleverer, then struggling against the president of the Council of the North, was there to be found anything like 'a true Yorkshireman, stout for the good of his country'. (Ironically, Foulis was in fact a comparative newcomer to Yorkshire. His was the special enthusiasm of the convert.)[4]

Reproaches like this could be very effective because they were directed at men close to their history and sensitive to the reputation of their homeland—the local community, a county, or even a hundred. Though Stuart England was perhaps more of a unity than most European countries, few men welcomed central control and for many it was a badge of servitude. They deplored the fact that so much government energy and money were spent on trying to recon-cile them to central policies in the name of economy and efficiency. Some of them were aware of similar activities on the continent and saw in conflicts between would-be absolute monarchies and centri-fugalism a mirror of their own situation. In France the struggle of the Huguenots against Richelieu certainly had provincial overtones. The Revolt of the Netherlands had been a reaction against the streamlining policies of the Hapsburgs, and the United Provinces, its unexpected outcome, might in the seventeenth century just as

[3] John Oglander, *A Royalist's Notebook,* ed. F. Bamford (1936), pp. 60–61.
[4] J. Rushworth, *Historical Collections* (1659–1701), ii. 216.

well have been called 'the Disunited Provinces'. In the Spains, Aragon and Catalonia, to say nothing of Portugal, responded still to the same fierce local sentiments. The Thirty Years' War in Germany takes on meaning when seen as part of the age-old competition between particularism and imperialism, a special form of centralization. In Prussia, Austria and Italy, everywhere provinces proved intractable and it would be a mistake to stress the destruction of ancient traditions, even in countries with standing armies. But the attempts were being made and Englishmen found them ominous as Tudor efforts to make the royal writ run freely throughout the realm were taken up, naturally enough, by their successors.

The Stuarts continued the councils in the north and in the Marches of Wales to deal immediately with the peculiar problems of the remoter regions. Temporary expedients to start with, these councils grew into elaborate institutions indispensible in tackling endemic provincial disorders. Their actions were clogged by writs of prohibition from the wary common law courts but equally by internal dissension. Their members were often local men whose aspirations might not readily coincide with the crown's. Their presidents, ostensibly impartial representatives of the state, sometimes became or were already deeply involved on their own account in local politics, so that their enemies could plausibly accuse them of usurping the royal trust to serve private ends. The Earl of Strafford, a northerner, found his authority as president of the Council of the North impugned by his own colleagues. Sir Thomas Gower blithely insulted his attorney in open court, and Henry Bellasis showed blatant contempt. He came into a room where the president was at a solemn meeting 'without showing any particular reverence . . . as in civility and duty he ought to have done', standing 'with his hat on his head, looking full upon his Lordship without stirring his hat, or using any other reverence. . . '. Later he was quite as insolent to the privy council itself.[5]

Strafford had trouble again from Sir David Foulis who publicly told the sheriff of Yorkshire to ignore a summons from the council, of which he was himself a member. It was, he argued, 'a paper court and the Lord President and his council have done more than they

[5] *ibid.*, ii. 88.

can justify in sending for you, a high sheriff'. If he were sheriff he would not care 'a dog's turd' for a body that had no power over even a mere J.P., who was 'above the Council at York'. A J.P. held an office confirmed by statute, but the council could appeal only to a commission for backing.[6]

The motives of Bellasis and Foulis were clearly a mixture of localism and personal animosity. Strafford himself told the privy council that

> upon these oppositions and others of like nature all rests are up, and the issue joined. . . . A provincial court at York or none? It is surely the state of the question, the very mark they shoot at; all eyes are at gaze there, and every ear listening here what becomes of it.

So unless the council had its own coercive power to compel the parties in a dispute to obey its decrees it would become '*bruta fulmina*, fruitless to the people, useless to the king. . . '. He himself would be 'altogether unable to govern and contain within the bounds of sobriety a people sometimes so stormy' as lived under its jurisdiction.[7] His determination to get control laid him open to 'calumny and hatred' but he was quite prepared for that. As he told his friend the Earl of Carlisle he was not 'so indulgent to my own ease, as to see [the king's] affairs suffer shipwreck whilst I myself rest secure in harbour'. He would rather put out to sea, ride out the storm and be found dead with the rudder still in his hands:

> All that I shall desire is that his Majesty and my other friends should narrowly observe me and see if ever I question any man in my own interests, but where [these] are only interlaced as accessories, his Majesty's service and the just aspect towards the public and duty of my place set before them as principals.[8]

Strafford was always at his most eloquent in denying a personal

[6] *ibid.*, ii. 218.
[7] State Papers Domestic ccxxvi, 1. Abstracted in *Calendar of State Papers Domestic, 1632*, pp. 450–1, and quoted in S. R. Gardiner, *History of England* (1894), vii. 238.
[8] Forster Mss., South Kensington Museum, quoted in Gardiner, *ibid.*, vii. 235.

interest, but his opponents may perhaps be forgiven for thinking that sometimes he protested too much. Anyway, they did not find more palatable the public principles he professed, which amounted to ever-encroaching control from the centre.

The north and Wales were, of course, areas with particular problems. But the rest of the country was not much more amenable to central authority. Local patriotism flourished on the very threshold of London, indeed within the City itself, which was a proud, even truculent, entity. Everywhere men used the word 'country' where we would say 'county'. When Kentishmen spoke of their country, they meant not this England, but this Kent, even this west, this east Kent. When Walter Mantell spoke as he lay dying of breathing once again the air of his beloved country, he wanted Kentish, not any old English air. In Dorset, Somerset and Lancashire, it was local rather than national politics that men revelled in—the rise and fall of families, such-and-such a match, that unheard-of setback at the polls. Parliamentary elections even in 1640, in 1660 or in 1689, were local excitements, never general. Rebellions, including the Great Rebellion itself, were emphatically local movements. This was fortunate for governments since it meant that outbreaks could usually be isolated, as was Penruddock's rising against Cromwell in the south-west in 1655. Actual revolt was, of course, occasional, but localism expressed itself in everyday affairs, directly against central authority, but also in inter-community squabbles. There were demarcation disputes over the maintenance of highways and bridges, which cost money, and had the added disadvantage of linking up two or more local units for a more than local purpose. Against the feelings that produced these effects arguments based on efficiency or convenience beat in vain.

To combat localism the crown had weapons, for example, the prerogative court of Star Chamber and its ecclesiastical twin, High Commission. There were also the judges of assize, ideally a two-way channel for the transmission of policy from the centre and of information back from the localities. Their function was well set out for them by Lord Keeper Finch as they started their weary rounds in the critical year of 1640. He began by stressing the unseemly behaviour of subordinate magistrates who sought popularity, 'diving into the people's hearts with kisses, offerings and fawnings'. The judges were to stop this. They were to insist on their own right to reverence. As they were the king's representatives, disrespect to them was an insult to the throne itself. Sometimes sheriffs and J.P.s could hardly be got to execute any processes at all, looking through their fingers, seeing what and whom they pleased, 'sometimes for reward, partiality and affection, or fear of offending great ones, or of offending a multitude'. The judges must report these delinquents so that they might be shuffled out of the commission of the peace. For Finch, the judges were 'the great surveyors of the kingdom on whom lesser officers should wait as on the king himself. But he had ruefully to confess that, in fact, few local authorities did give their attendance.

> What humour they are of that think themselves too good to serve the king, I know not, but let them know it is in no man's choice whether he will serve the king in the ministry of justice or no.

Magistrates who had local and personal motives for seeking office must be brought to understand their duty to king and commonwealth.[9]

All this was put with eloquence and vigour. But Finch said nothing new. For more than a century his predecessors had bemoaned that 'such careless and slothful men do daily colour and cloak their faults with the title of quietness'.[10] At best the judges could act as a slipping brake on localism, and as they sometimes went year after year on the same circuit they might get to know the magnates so well that they were not even that. Moreover, even J.P.s who were anxious to do their duties came to resent trite lectures by visiting judges followed by submission to 'the mercy of the Council Table'.[11] Sir Peter Temple, sheriff for Buckinghamshire in 1634, had worked hard to bring in ship money. Yet when his term of office was up the privy council still harassed him. In 1636, lying ill in London and 'taking physic', he was sent for by the king. He found himself saddled not only with his own alleged defaults but with those

[9] Rushworth, iii. 985–8.
[10] Simonds D'Ewes, *Journals of All the Parliaments of Queen Elizabeth* (1682), p. 33.
[11] *Calendar of Wynn (of Gwydir) Papers, 1515–1690*, ed. National Library of Wales (1926), p. 270.

of his successor. He was put in the hands of a royal messenger and 'compelled with all the distresses and imprisonings that may be imposed upon the country'. Soon there would be another interview with the king and 'as he likes my proceedings I am to continue in the messenger's hands or be released—or worse.' No wonder he complained that his life was 'nothing but toil and hath been for many years'.[12] Yet he was only one of many who had reason to fear a smart punishment. A well-argued report by the sheriff of Lincoln for 1640, John Brownlow, setting out his difficulties in collecting ship money, was returned with these impatient phrases scrawled across it: 'His excuses are frivolous . . . he is to execute the writ or answer for his own neglect.'[13]

This heavy-handedness, which seems to have grown under the personal rule of Charles I, led to something like a standstill of local officials in 1640. This was, indirectly at least, one of the compelling reasons for summoning the Long Parliament. Everywhere gentlemen were refusing to become J.P.s, or were resigning, or were being purged for remissness. Nine solid men who had held office in Somerset were elected to the parliament of November 1640. All backed the popular programme that swept away Star Chamber, High Commission and the councils in the north and in Wales. All but one voted for the attainder and execution of Strafford. It is clear that they recognized in him and his clerical ally, William Laud, dangerous advocates of national unity through uniformity, men quite unfit for the state of England as they knew it and liked it. Administrators are always inclined to overrate the attractions of efficiency.

The difficulties of central government did not disappear with a change of régime. The problems of parliament, Commonwealth and Protectorate turned out to be much the same as those of Charles I. During the Civil War, parliament set up county committees of local men to act as its representatives and agents. True to type, they acted as much in what they thought were the interests of their own localities as they did for the state itself. They collected money efficiently enough, but were reluctant to send it up to the central finance committee in London. They found too many uses for it nearer home.

[12] Lord Nugent, *Memorials of John Hampden* (4th edn., 1860), p. 105.
[13] *Cal. State Papers Domestic, 1640*, pp. 327–8.

Like the old authorities they, too, could be both apathetic and inventive, turning a blind eye to one local problem while coping thoughtfully with another. Some of their members used their ill-defined authority to pursue local feuds, very much as their predecessors had done in peacetime. Quarrels between leading committee-men led to or reflected factions among the gentry. Towards the end of the war 'mean' men, new to political responsibility but given a chance to exercise it by unusual circumstances, became more important on the county committees. Such men tended to overlook the claims of localism in their enthusiasm for the wider demands of the common cause. But some even of these relapsed to older ways. It was not easy to keep up with what was going on at the highest levels and the maintenance of their own personal positions might depend more on good relations with neighbours than on the favour of the parties momentarily on top at Westminster. Even the Levellers, whose stress on the unity of a sovereign people marks them out as nationally-minded, were not oblivious to the claims of localism. In 1647 Richard Overton, making *An Appeal from the degenerate Representative Body the Commons of England*, urged the army to press that

> every County may have liberty to choose some certain number amongst themselves, to inquire into and present to the Parliament, what might be the just Laws, Customs, and Privileges of each County, and that those County Commissioners be bound to receive all and every impeachment and impeachments, by any person or persons whatsoever, of the respective Counties, against any of their own respective Knights or Burgesses in Parliament, for falsifying and betraying his or their County's trust, or in any wise endeavouring the introduction of an arbitrary power in the Land.

Other articles demanded decentralization of justice and 'free election' of all local officials by the people. If these and other demands had been met there would have been the creation of something like a welfare polity based on the localities rather than the state itself.[14]

[14] *Leveller Manifestoes of the Puritan Revolution,* ed. D. M. Wolfe (New York, 1944), pp. 189–90.

Failing to establish a workable form of government with the support of new-fangled parliaments, Oliver Cromwell decided in 1655 to impose another age of 'Thorough'. Following Penruddock's rising the whole country was divided into a dozen areas, each under a major-general. Their job was to supervise the county committees and J.P.s, all local authorities in fact, new or old, cutting across established administrative boundaries and newly 'cantonizing' England.[15] (Incidentally, Edward Hyde had used the word 'canton' in 1640 in condemning the Council of the North, that grievance of the 'vexed, worn people of the North' which yet 'by the logic and consequence of it is the grievance of the whole kingdom'.)[16] Instructions were given to the major-generals to implement efficient and uniform rule from the centre, wider in scope and by virtue of the sword greater in potential even than that of 1629–40. Besides keeping an eye on political dissidents who might flourish by the laxity of local officials, they were to inform themselves of 'all idle and loose people who have no visible way of livelihood, nor calling nor employment'. The poor laws were to be effectually executed. There must be full reporting back. All this has a very familiar air. But there was something extra. Social and economic stability was to be reinforced by a moral reformation. The major-generals were 'by their constant carriage and conversation to promote godliness and virtue and discourage profaneness and ungodliness'. Inferior authorities were to be pressed to effect acts and ordinances against drunkenness, swearing, plays, interludes, sabbath-breaking 'and such like wickedness and abominations'.[17]

The major-generals certainly worked hard in the interests of the central power but they could not easily avoid getting mixed up in local politics themselves. Either way they were resented. The reaction was seen in elections for parliament in 1656 and in that parliament itself, which in effect voted the system out of existence. The major-general for Kent, Hezekiah Kelsey, complained that at Maidstone there was a sad spirit against whatever good the govern-

[15] *The Parliamentary Diary of Thomas Burton*, ed. J. T. Rutt (1828), i. 315.
[16] Rushworth, ii. 162–5.
[17] *Writings and Speeches of Oliver Cromwell*, ed. W. C. Abbott, (Cambridge, Mass., 1937–47), iii. 844–8.

ment tried to do. Cavaliers were ready to sink differences with Presbyterians to oppose the state. Most of those chosen for parliament would be bitter against 'swordsmen, decimators, courtiers' and would work for 'blood and confusion'. Above all they would 'down with major-generals'. Kelsey thought that to preserve them there must be a resolution at the centre which in the event was lacking.[18] To save his foreign policy and get other reforms, Cromwell had to abandon the 'cantons'. Both the personal government of Charles I and the rule of the major-generals, worse because it was armed, were swept away by the spirited resistance of local communities facing a common menace.

The major-generals with their new model militia were only the latest in a long line of attempts to make defence truly national and effective. It is in this sphere that the inhibiting effect of the parochial outlook of the counties is most marked. Charles I had frequently expressed his displeasure at the great neglect of musters. He could not afford, financially or politically, a standing army like those of his continental cousins. So he worked for 'a perfect militia' with regular training and exercises with arms, 'of the modern fashion', and with well-maintained beacons and magazines.[19] Among his ministers Strafford was prepared if need be to 'wink at the law' in such matters.[20] There was little support from the localities. They continued to look askance at action outside their own borders, even in the crisis of war with the Scots in 1639–40. The trained bands of Dorset refused to cross the county line and murdered their officer. In Kent weapons supplied at the expense of the community fell to pieces. The deputies there reported 'a stubborn sullennesss' among the men called out.

> In short, we find a confusion, some will not go beyond their colours, others will not go into Scotland, all are yeomen and farmers who say they must be as assuredly undone by going as refusing.[21]

[18] *Cal. State Papers Domestic, 1656–7,* p. 87.
[19] T. G. Barnes, *Somerset, 1625–40* (1961), p. 224; *Wynn Papers,* p. 253.
[20] Tanner Mss. lxxii, 300, quoted in Gardiner, *History,* vii. 27–8.
[21] *Cal. State Papers Domestic, 1640,* p. 148.

The Civil War, precipitated by the problem of where to lodge control of armed force, began with a competition between crown and parliament for command of the ramshackle militia. In the war itself, fighting on both sides was hampered by intensified localism. This feeling was responsible for abortive pacts of neutrality in several counties and for the comparative enthusiasm for local garrison duty. Parliament tried to offset it by forging county associations. Certainly the Eastern Association made a big contribution to victory at Marston Moor, but the associations generally proved an unsteady base for permanent success. They were at length replaced by the nationally and professionally organized New Model Army, whose troops refused to march away when war was over. Their unsightly presence encouraged a hatred of standing armies that survived the Restoration and helped to whistle James II, for whom the militia was 'not sufficient', out of three kingdoms.[22]

After 1660 the power of the state was still limited by the legislation of 1641 which had cleared away so many engines for coercing the provinces. Like the various régimes of the interregnum, the restored monarchy had cause to regret that glad clean sweep. Charles II and James II tried to remedy their situation by remodelling borough charters, purging the local benches and reviving something like the old High Commission. But provincialism won in the revolution of 1689. Its triumph had some curious effects. On the one hand it meant negligence, apathy, even downright corruption. But it also brought flexibility and chances to be seized by community-minded men to experiment and to do in their little local 'countries' what a later age might copy for the nation itself.

Books for further reading

T. G. Barnes, *Somerset, 1625–1640: a County's Government during the 'Personal Rule'* (1961).

M. Coate, *Cornwall in the Great Civil War* (2nd edn., 1963).

[22] *Journals of the House of Commons,* xi. 756.

A. H. Dodd, *Studies in Stuart Wales* (1953).

J. H. Elliott, *The Revolt of the Catalans* (1963).

A. M. Everitt, *Suffolk and the Great Rebellion, 1640–1660* (Suffolk Records Society, 1960).

A. M. Everitt, *The Community of Kent and the Great Rebellion, 1640–1660* (1966).

R. Howell, *Newcastle upon Tyne and the Puritan Revolution* (1967).

M. F. Keeler, *The Long Parliament, 1640–1641* (Philadelphia, 1954).

S. Kliger, *The Goths in England* (Cambridge, Mass., 1952).

E. M. Leonard, *The Early History of English Poor Relief* (Cambridge, 1900; 2nd. imp. London, 1965).

D. H. Pennington and I. A. Roots (eds.), *The Committee at Stafford, 1643–1645* (1957).

R. R. Reid, *The King's Council in the North* (1921).

W. B. Willcox, *Gloucestershire: a Study in Local Government, 1590–1640* (New Haven, 1940).

III

The County Community

ALAN EVERITT

When the Long Parliament, the parliament of the English Revolution, met in 1640, it did not meet as a body of revolutionaries. It met first and foremost as a body of angry countrymen. When the knights and squires who represented the counties and boroughs of England came up to Westminster from their estates in Cumberland or Cornwall or Kent, they did not come with the intention of creating a new world; they came to restore an old one. Wistfully, but resolutely, they looked back to what seemed in retrospect the golden age of Queen Elizabeth. What they resented most, as Ivan Roots suggests elsewhere in this volume, was not simply the illegal levy of ship money, or the Arminianism of Archbishop Laud, but the increasing interference of the central government in the life of those little local worlds which they had left behind them at home. In a few months the abuses would be reformed, and then they would return to their native counties and govern them once again as they alone knew how to. There was nothing revolutionary in this attitude of mind. What was new was the Country's lack of confidence in the Court, and the absence of anything at the centre which could sublimate local loyalty into loyalty to the state. With the death of the great Queen, the Court had rapidly been taken over by cliques of hated upstarts like the Duke of Buckingham. And as its influence over the nation as a whole declined, each region, each county, became more than ever before a little self-centred kingdom on its own.

There is nothing surprising in the localism of provincial people, which, as Ivan Roots explains, brought the king's government to a grinding halt in 1640. We may think it misguided; but it seems surprising only because so much of our history, until recent years, has been written from the viewpoint of Westminster, or the stance of untypical minorities like the Levellers and Laudians. As soon as one begins to study the history of any provincial community as a whole, whether it is one of the forty counties of England, like Suffolk and Kent, or one of the 750 market towns, like Leicester and Northampton, one finds that even during the Civil War the shouting and the tumult of these minorities played only a small part in its history. Most towns and counties were far more interested in living a life of their own, in which politics played merely an intermittent part, than in supporting either roundheads or cavaliers. Of course they had not been unaffected by the far-reaching changes of the preceding century in England as a whole. One of the greatest of these changes, the expansion of London, had affected them in a variety of ways. The demands of its food market, the growth in the power of parliament, the increase in litigation, the scintillation of court-life, the rage for 'conspicuous consumption', the sophistication of manners, the efflorescence of Stuart culture: all these developments had intensified the attractive power of London over the minds and movements of many provincial people. Yet the impact of London was not universally diffused throughout English society. Locally it was intense, particularly in influencing food production, as in the Thames valley and the Isle of Thanet. But in most of the countryside it was only occasionally felt, if it was felt at all. It was only a limited number of country people who were directly affected by it: small groups of commercially-minded farmers on one hand, and of courtiers, cavaliers, members of parliament, and ne'er-do-wells on the other. Despite all the noisy proclamations of the Stuarts banishing the gentry back to their native counties, probably at least three provincial squires in four rarely or never visited the metropolis. In the county of Kent, out of more than 800 gentry in the shire in 1640, about twenty possessed London houses, another twenty sat in parliament, and thirty or forty, at the most, became courtiers or cavaliers. Beyond a radius of fifteen miles from the city, the vast majority of Kentish people were dyed-in-the-wool countrymen: living, marrying, farming, buying, selling, governing, hunting, and visiting within a very limited circle of local manor-houses and market towns.

This attachment of provincial people to their native county—or country as they often called it—sometimes comes to light in the comments they made when visiting London. At other times they rarely referred to their local loyalties directly, because no society gives utterance to its deepest assumptions until they have begun to be challenged. But when a small country landowner, like Henry Oxinden of Great Maydeacon in East Kent, visited the capital—in his case the only visit of his life—he at once felt himself an exile there, and looked upon the vast, incredible city of a quarter of a million people with a sort of fascinated horror. Henry Oxinden was far from being the drunken backwoods squire of political legend. He was in fact a competent classicist and a voluminous poet. But the circle of his interests lay wholly elsewhere than in London; and while he was there he wrote a series of revealing letters to his wife, whom he had left behind him in Kent to look after his estates, while he attended a wearisome suit at law:

> I will make all the haste I can to thee, taking no more pleasure in being at London than in being amongst my enemies. . . . I wish my business at an end that I might come home and see after my harvest, fearing I may receive prejudice by my absence. . . . I am fain to trudge up and down all day from morning to night. . . . If I can once get clear of it [London], I never desire to come again to it. . . . Dear Heart, this is only to let thee know how infinitely I long to be with thee.[1]

No wonder Henry Oxinden was so relieved to return home again a few weeks later and to take up his country pursuits again.

It was families like the Oxindens who formed the backbone of most of the local opposition to Charles I in the 'thirties and to parliament in the Civil War. It was they who headed the county community. For a time, after the formation of the New Model Army in 1645, their power seemed to go into eclipse. Yet in Kent, at least, the county community achieved its most spectacular triumph after that date, in one of the many local insurrections of 1648. The astonishing Kentish rebellion of that year can be called the last of the great local risings in English history. Its origins and its aims were almost entirely

[1] British Museum, Add. Ms. 28002, ff. 174, 306, 311, 317, 320, 342.

confined to the shire. Its leaders refused to negotiate with their neighbours in Essex, Sussex, and Surrey. Virtually the whole county was directly or indirectly engaged in this rising, and contemporaries themselves were amazed by its suddenness. Beneath the apparent submission of the county to parliament, however, the hidden leaven of opposition had in fact been working for years among the influential families who had been excluded by parliament from the government of the shire, but whose territorial and patriarchal influence still controlled its loyalties. This was how an outsider, the Norfolk Royalist Roger L'Estrange, described the insurrection:

> In a straggling disarmed county, within two days' march of an experienced, successful army, under the very nose of the county militia, . . . they made in 12 days 12,000 men effective, . . . gave an amuse and diversion to their adversaries, . . . gave themselves the glory of beginning an action wherein the whole nation stood at gaze and durst not second them. They made war *alone* upon the masters . . . of three kingdoms. . . . Our age produces not anywhere persons . . . of a more primitive worthiness than in Kent.[2]

Why was it that this kind of county feeling was so prevalent in the seventeenth century? The answer lies in the social structure and the historical development of the county community. In every English shire there was a group of native families at the heart of local society who had, as it were, grown up out of the soil of the county with the passing of the centuries. Their numbers and origins varied greatly, of course, from shire to shire. The claims of some of them to be of Norman descent were almost always pure mythology, but they often did date back to the thirteenth century. Many of them had originated as small freeholders, sometimes taking their names from the settlements they had carved out of the waste. In some counties, like Northamptonshire, this nucleus of ancient local gentry was small and weak, and of course there were newcomers in varying numbers amongst the gentry in every English county. But in much of the north, the west, and the south of England, the oligarchy of

[2] Roger L'Estrange, *L'Estrange his Vindication to Kent: and the Justification of Kent to the World* (1649), n.p.

indigenous families was very powerful, and it was impossible to rule the shires without its support.

In Kent, an intensely conservative county at this date, it certainly was. The part of the county near London had long been affected by economic and social change; but the vast majority of the gentry lived well away from the capital, on the downlands of East Kent, the chartlands in the middle of the county, or the sandstone hills of the Weald. Around Canterbury and Sandwich, about sixty or seventy miles from London, 85 per cent of the local gentry had been settled in the locality since well before the end of the fifteenth century. In the Wealden parishes between Tenterden and Brenchley the proportion was higher still. Many of the names of these local families—Oxinden, Twysden, Amherst, Bathurst, Denne, Honywood, Hardres, and Horsmonden—indicate the local places where they had originated. Few of them had suddenly risen to fortune during their long history; most of them had grown up gradually with the centuries, like the houses they lived in.

Unlike the Jacobean palaces of the newer gentry in counties like Northamptonshire, most of these Kentish manor-houses were somewhat patchwork affairs: modest in scale, medieval in origin, rambling in plan, added to bit by bit by each generation, inseparable from the life of the families who owned them. Even the great Elizabethan houses of Kent, like Knole and Penshurst, were essentially medieval in plan and structure. For this reason Kentish houses and estates bred in their owners a kind of conservatism, a sense of continuity with the past of the whole county, which it seemed positively sacrilegious to ignore. Ben Jonson sensed something of this when he visited the Sidneys at Penshurst:

> Thou art not, Penshurst, built to envious show
> Of touch or marble, nor canst boast a row
> Of polished pillars or a roof of gold;
> Thou hast no lantern whereof tales are told,
> Or stair, or courts; but stand'st an ancient pile,
> And these grudged at, art reverenced the while.
> Thou joy'st in better marks, of soil, of air,
> Of wood, of water: therein thou art fair. . . .

And though thy walls be of the country stone,
They're reared with no man's ruin, no man's groan;
There's none that dwell about them wish them down;
But all come in, the farmer and the clown,
And no one empty-handed, to salute
Thy lord and lady, though they have no suit.[3]

Jonson's lines may be idyllic, but the basis of the kind of life he described was entirely practical and hard-headed. These manor-houses, in Kent or any other county, were also farmhouses, rooted in the fields around them. England was still an agrarian country, and families like the Oxindens and Twysdens in Kent, or the Barnardistons in Suffolk, knew every field and wood and hedgerow on their estate, and frequently attended their local fairs and markets at Canterbury, Maidstone, or Bury St. Edmunds. One of the most useful farming account-books of the seventeenth century belongs to the redoubtable Kentish squire, Nicholas Toke, of Godinton Park near Ashford. Godinton Park itself still survives, and the money for much of its embellishment came from Toke's extremely successful farming around Godinton and in Romney Marsh. Similarly Sir George Sondes, in Charles I's reign, rebuilt the lovely mansion of Lees Court, on the Downs a few miles north of Godinton, largely from the profits of cattle-raising and corn-farming. This is how he describes his husbandry in this fertile area:

> My lands were all well-stocked. I had at least one hundred head of great cattle, half a hundred horses, and those none of the worst, some of them being worth forty or fifty pounds apiece. I had five hundred sheep, besides other stock; about a thousand quarters of wheat and malt in granaries, and ten barns (none of the least) all full of good corn, and great quantities of flax and hops.[4]

If it was the gradual rise of the Kentish squirearchy from humble origins, and the agrarian basis of their fortunes, that rooted so many

---

[3] *Ben Jonson,* ed. C. H. Herford, Percy and Evelyn Simpson (1947), viii. 93–5.
[4] *Sir George Sondes his Plain Narrative to the World of all Passages upon the Death of his two Sons* (1655), printed in *Harleian Miscellany* (1813), x. 65.

of these families in their native parishes, it was their frequent inter-marriage with one another that united them into a single county community. By 1640 it had long been customary for them to marry, as a rule, amongst the daughters of local gentry. Some of the wealthier magnates married in London, or further afield, but the great majority necessarily found their brides amongst neigh-bouring families. More than three-quarters of the gentry of East Kent married into other Kentish families. In the Midlands the proportion was not so high, but in Wales and the west country it may well have been even higher than in Kent.

Not surprisingly, this greatly strengthened the sense of local cohesion amongst the gentry. In some shires, by 1640, virtually all the county families could have been incorporated into a single family tree. When Mary Honywood died in Kent in 1620, at the age of 93, there can have been few local families unrelated to her 367 descen-dants. The old proverb 'in Kent they are all first cousins' was scarcely an exaggeration. Nor were these ties merely nominal. There was often a strong sense of family responsibility towards quite remote dependants. This is how Sir Thomas Peyton described his household at Knowlton Court, on the downs between Sandwich and Dover, after his sister's death:

> She has left me seven children, all young, who have no surviving friend but myself. I have another sister who expects every day to be a widow with nine children. My wife and myself have eight children to employ our most dear and natural care about. I have a brother unfortunately married, who together with his wife and six small children are supported almost totally by myself, and whose callings and livelihood I must inevitably provide for. I have half sisters and brothers who live by my support, and nephews and nieces who together with their children have all their support and maintenance from my direction.[5]

An intimate picture of another Kentish household is given in Sir George Sondes's autobiographical writings. From these it is clear that the responsibilities of the family head were not restricted to caring for sons, daughters, and kinsmen, but extended also to servants

[5] British Museum, Add. Ms. 44846, f. 69ᵛ.

in the manor-house, and labourers and tenants on the estate. Sir George was a staunch Anglican, and his sense of family duty was rooted in deep religious conviction as well as in unquestioning local tradition:

> I am sure no man's house in the country of Kent is more open to poor and rich than mine. . . . As it is, I am sure there are twenty poor people at least weekly relieved, and that more than once. . . . I never arrested or imprisoned any tenant for his rent, nor willingly used any severe course, if I could indifferently be satisfied any other way. . . . [In] ordering my family and duties thereto belonging, I confess it is an excellent thing when a man can say, 'I and my house do and will serve the Lord.' . . . It is the master's part to see them perform the outward duties of God's service, as prayer and going to church, and shew them the way by his own godly example; this I was always mindful of, frequenting the church on the Lord's day, both forenoon and afternoon . . . and calling upon my servants to do the same. And all the week after, it was my constant course to pray with my family once, if not twice every day; and if I had not a [chaplain] in my house, I performed the office myself.[6]

In a society where families like the Peytons and Sondeses linked the community together, it was no myth for the gentry to regard themselves as a single family. Naturally this did not mean that they lived in unruffled harmony. In every family there are feuds and quarrels, and they are often fiercest where family feeling is most intense. But the frequent appeals in all parts of England, during the Civil War, to 'the love and unity of the county' were not mere hypocrisy. Family division, when it came for so many in 1642, often caused acute distress, and did so precisely because the sense of community was powerful. In Kent family loyalty frequently mollified the antagonism of party division. Many of the gentry on opposite sides continued to correspond and to meet one another, and still permitted their sons and daughters to intermarry. In a few counties the sense of kinship was sufficient to outweigh many political misgivings and prevent division. This was certainly not true in midland

---

[6] *Harleian Miscellany*, x. 49–51.

areas like Leicestershire, already torn by family feuds before the Civil War began. Nor was it altogether true in Kent. But it was true in Suffolk, where the county was headed by the ancient Barnardiston family of Kedington.

Under the leadership of Sir Nathaniel Barnardiston, the great father-figure of the county, the gentry of Suffolk were virtually united in their support of parliament in every major political decision they had to take between 1640 and 1660. Only a small group of cavaliers and recusants as a rule dissented. A contemporary biographical account of Sir Nathaniel describes how he governed his own large household, and by implication the whole community of Suffolk:

> Consider him as *pater familias*, the governor and master of a family: . . . he had at one time ten or more such servants of that eminency for piety and sincerity, that I never yet saw their like at one time in any family in the nation. . . . Towards his children he executed the office of an heavenly father to their souls . . . and many times he would take them into his closet, and there pray over them, and for them. If at any time they had offended him, so singular was his moderation and wisdom toward them, that he would never reprove them, much less correct them in his displeasure, but still waited the most convenient time, until which time they seldom discerned that he was angry by any other effect but his silence.[7]

No doubt this picture of Sir Nathaniel is idealized, but his authoritarian influence was certainly responsible for the fact that the county was relatively united. This is how Robert Reyce, another Suffolk man, described the county in 1618:

> The gentry of Suffolk meet often, conversing most familiarly together, which so winneth the goodwill one of another with all reverent regard of the meaner sort, and true love and unfeigned affection of their neighbours, that if differences do arise, which are very seldom, such is the great discretion ever tempered with love and kindness among them, that these divisions are soon smothered and appeased. Such is the religious unity wherewith in all good

[7] Samuel Fairclough, *The Saint's Worthiness* . . . (1653), pp. 17–18.

actions they do concur, that whatsoever offendeth one offendeth all, and whosoever satisfieth one contenteth all.[8]

The growing power of the county community, and of patriarchal households like the Barnardistons who composed it, was only one of the far-reaching social developments of the period. There were other economic influences working against the insularity of these communities. As we have already seen, in Northamptonshire the nucleus of ancient local gentry was small, and there were newcomers in varying degrees amongst the gentry of every English county. Generally speaking the new blood was absorbed into the old society without transforming it so completely as in Northampton-shire; but in this county, in the heart of the midlands, a great deal of enclosure had taken place under the Tudors, and tracts of ancient royal forest had been granted out to newcomers. In 1640, barely a quarter of the 335 local gentry in Northamptonshire had been resident in the county before 1500, and more than a third had settled there since the death of Queen Elizabeth. The superb country houses for which the county is famous today were in fact almost all built in the late sixteenth and seventeenth centuries, whilst their owners were relative newcomers. In a well-known passage William Camden graphically described the shire at the time when these palaces were rising in it, and while the new gentry were still engaged in the highly commercialized corn and sheep-farming operations on which their fortunes were often based:

It is an open country, very populous, and everywhere adorned with noblemen's and gentlemen's houses; and very full of towns and churches. . . . Its soil, both for tillage and pasture, is ex-ceedingly fertile; but it is not well-stocked with wood. But everywhere . . . it is filled and as it were beset with sheep; which . . . used to be so gentle, and fed with so little; but now, as it is reported, begin to be so ravenous and wild, that they devour men, and waste and depopulate fields, houses, and towns.[9]

[8] Robert Reyce, *Suffolk in the XVIIth Century: the Breviary of Suffolk by Robert Reyce, 1618*, ed. Lord Francis Hervey (1902), p. 60.

[9] William Camden, *Britannia, or a Chorographical Description of Great Britain and Ireland*, ed. Edmund Gibson (1753), i. col. 511.

The story of these new families in Northamptonshire is in fact a
classic example of the 'rise of the gentry' between 1540 and 1640.
Camden's observations are confirmed by those of another, rather
more jaundiced, local observer in 1641:

> The number of nobility and gentry is greatly overgrown. Now
> there is increased a very great number, more especially since the
> beginning of King James. . . . They did rise upon the church
> lands and possessions, being seated for the most part upon the
> abbeys and such like houses taken from bishops and churches . . .
> which raised a number of pettifoggers and many new gentle-
> men. . . . And it is easy to be observed that, whereas in Queen
> Elizabeth's time there was but two or three knights in the shire,
> now there is sixty, besides many pretended esquires and gentle-
> men, which, as Bacon saith, do spend much and earn little, living
> for the most part above their quality and degree, which they
> ought to keep in all their behaviour, expenses, and apparel.[10]

Complaints of this kind were, of course, the familiar stock-in-
trade of old-fashioned moralists in all parts of England. The significant fact is that in Northamptonshire, though exaggerated, they
were unusually near the truth. Whereas in Kent the indigenous
oligarchy was powerful enough to absorb the few outsiders without
any fundamental change in its own outlook, in Northamptonshire
the new gentry largely displaced the old, retained few links with the
past, and formed a new ascendancy of their own. Quite naturally
this new society was on the whole more sympathetic to the advanced
ideas of the age than in Kent. Its members were rarely enthusiastic
about subordinating county loyalty to loyalty to the state, but they
gradually came to see the necessity of it. They did not share the
tradition of compromise and insularity which came naturally to a
community whose local roots ran deep and whose ideas were
decidedly patriarchal and provincial. There was not the same urge
amongst them to come to terms with the established order as there
was in areas where the more ancient gentry were in unquestioned
control. Their radicalism was greatly strengthened, moreover, by

---

[10] *A Certificate from Northamptonshire* (1641 [?2]), pp. 17–18.

that of the borough of Northampton, the county town and garrison in which so many of them took refuge during the Civil War.

Quite as important as the influx of new gentry in counties like Northamptonshire was the immense expansion in internal trade in this period, and the emergence of a virtually new kind of society, that of the wayfaring traders and merchants, who controlled it. In the long run, this development was probably more important in transforming the provincial world than the establishment of new local dynasties. Once the latter had struck local roots and married among themselves for two or three generations, they tended to harden into another local caste as rigid as the old; whereas the community of wayfaring merchants always remained mobile, rootless, and radical, questing in its ambitions and continually addicted to change. The great period of emergence of these migrant traders began about 1570. They were not an altogether new phenomenon in English history, of course. There are obvious traces of their activities in Chaucer, for instance, and they played an important part in the great cloth trade of the later middle ages. But between 1570 and 1640 there were far greater numbers of wayfaring merchants in England than ever before, buying and selling all kinds of goods, and travelling all over the country from Cumberland to Kent. They bought and sold their goods, often in very large quantities, usually on credit, and principally at fairs or in the great inns of the major provincial towns, like Exeter, Northampton, and York. Wherever they went they were specialists in the particular commodity they dealt in: some in wool, some in cloth, others in hops, barley, cattle, horses, or sheep. Robert Reyce once again gives us a telling account of the busy hop-merchants of his native county of Suffolk in the early seventeenth century:

Whilst . . . the markets and fairs proved quick, and Stourbridge [Fair], London, and the western parts vented whatsoever this or any other country could bring forth, there sprung up a new company, some from London, some from other parts, called hop-merchants: these, prying into the last year's store then remaining, diligently hearkening from beyond the sea what likelihood there was from those parts, and carefully looking into every garden and hopyard here at home, in what towardness they stood, comparing the former year's experience with the time present, at length with themselves resolved and concluded of a price, who travelling into the country where these hops were, they offered to the owners at their own doors, either for those remaining or for new at the next gathering to come.[11]

As these wayfaring merchants travelled, year after year, they gradually came to form a distinct and self-conscious community on their own, sometimes meeting one another regularly at the same annual fairs, or in the same inns, and so developing their own sense of cohesion, and their own methods and ideals. As a consequence, the number and size of the trading inns in the greater provincial towns rapidly increased. A census of accommodation in the inns of England in 1686 shows that in Salisbury there were 548 beds and stables for 865 horses in the hostelries of the city. In Northampton the number of inns rose from a mere dozen in 1600 to more than fifty before the end of the century. Some of these hostelries had as many as thirty or forty rooms, and there were scores of smaller alehouses, which were frequented by sheep and cattle drovers from Wales and the north.

It is not difficult to see how the wayfaring life of England, which came to be concentrated in inland entrepôts like Northampton, tended to break down some of the local isolationism of the counties. In a certain sense the members of the wayfaring community became a kind of fifth column, travelling all over the kingdom, and broadcasting, as they went, the revolutionary ideas of the Independents and radicals before and during the Civil War. The vehement Puritanism of towns like Northampton was directly connected with their importance as centres of wayfaring life. It came quite naturally to the Puritan ministers of such places to picture the world to their hearers as no more than 'an inn, in our way to a better, an heavenly country'.[12] There was, indeed, a certain temperamental kinship

[11] Reyce, *The Breviary of Suffolk*, pp. 31–2.
[12] John Conant, *The Life of the Reverend and Venerable John Conant, D.D.* (1823), p. 77. The author, writing after 1660, plays down his father's Puritanism, but he had supported Cromwell and the Republican régime.

between the questing energy of these travelling merchants and the dynamism of the left-wing Puritanism of the Civil War.

It was the wayfaring traders, moreover, who were most hard-hit by the disruption of the inland trade of England during the Civil War, especially by Royalists plundering their goods on the midland roads. For economic as well as religious reasons, they became some of the king's most unyielding antagonists. Sometimes their complaints were reported in the Parliamentarian newspapers of the time:

> The Lord of Northampton hath surprised fifty-seven carriers' horses coming from Cheshire and other places laden with cheese and other commodities, to the great loss of the poor carriers . . . They write from Daventry that the people of that famous county of Northampton, understanding that the Earl of Northampton had been plundering of Daventry, and was carrying away the goods there and the poor carriers' horses and lading to Banbury, did rise in great numbers, sent out their scouts, and those met with the enemy's scouts, killed two of them, which made the other run to the Earl and tell him the Parliament's forces were coming, who no sooner understood it but he left all his booty and fled back to Banbury as fast as he could.[13]

Or take the words of Hugh Peter, the Independent minister, in a sermon preached shortly after the war. They illustrate how much the wayfaring community rejoiced in the victory of the New Model and welcomed the return of peace:

> Oh, the blessed change we see that can travel now from Edinburgh to the Land's End in Cornwall, who not long since were blocked up at our doors. To see the highways occupied again; to hear the carter whistling to his toiling team; to see the weekly carrier attend his constant mart; to see the hills rejoicing, the valleys laughing.[14]

But in the long run it was neither the Independents, whom the wayfaring community favoured, nor the cavaliers who were to

[13] *Special Passages and Certain Informations*, No. 24, Jan. 1642/3.
[14] Quoted from *God's Doing, Man's Duty*, p. 24, in C. V. Wedgwood, *The King's War, 1641–1647* (1958), p. 551.

decide the destinies of England. Both parties were minorities, small minorities, whose restless individualism ran counter to the far weightier patriarchal traditions, the settled, local, family life of the old provincial order. Both, in short, put party or personal loyalty above the claims of kinship. In the most famous book ever to come from an author connected with the community of travelling traders, *The Pilgrim's Progress*, this conflict of loyalties is dramatically illustrated in the opening pages. John Bunyan was himself a travelling tinker, and he must have known much about the wayfaring life of the big merchants of his native town of Bedford. By 1640 Bedford had developed into a major inland port and market, plying an extensive trade on the River Ouse to King's Lynn, importing coal from Newcastle, and exporting corn from the whole of the south-east midlands. It was quite natural, therefore, that Bunyan's great classic should tell the story of a journey—the journey of the solitary Christian pilgrim from this world to the next. Just as the wayfaring trader of the time was compelled, by the call of business, to leave his family behind him and travel alone for long weeks together from inn to inn and town to town, so when Bunyan's Christian was faced with a conflict of loyalty, the call of individual duty triumphed, and he had to leave wife and children behind him 'and he saw them no more'.

But this ideal, however noble, was alien to the deeply-rooted family structure of provincial life. Just as Charles I had been forced to govern through the patriarchal power of the county community in the sixteen-thirties, so in the end Cromwell too found it impossible to govern without its support. He could control it with the aid of the sword, but he could never change its genius. For the families who composed it were not all fighting merely for the selfish preservation of their own power. Undoubtedly many of them were doing so, of course. But as a whole they were also fighting for something more: for the preservation of a kind of society without which the world as they knew it—and as their tenants and labourers knew it—could not survive. For in the strange and introverted society of the county community everything—religion, learning, law, politics, trade, even history itself—was formed and tempered by the bonds of local kinship and custom. It was this that gave shape to the infinite diversity of English provincial life in the seventeenth century. How full of vigour and vitality it all was! Yet those of us who teach or write about it feel that we are only at the beginning of the exploration of it; only touching the borders of a vanished and enthralling world.

Books for further reading

T. G. Barnes, *Somerset, 1625–1640: a County's Government during the 'Personal Rule'* (1961).

M. Coate, *Cornwall in the Great Civil War* (2nd edn., 1963).

A. M. Everitt, *The Community of Kent and the Great Rebellion, 1640–60* (1966).

A. M. Everitt, 'The marketing of agricultural produce', in *The Agrarian History of England and Wales*, iv, 1500–1640, ed. Joan Thirsk (1967).

A. M. Everitt, *Suffolk and the Great Rebellion, 1640–1660* (Suffolk Records Society, 1960).

D. H. Pennington and I. A. Roots, eds., *The Committee at Stafford, 1643–1645.*

A. L. Rowse, *Tudor Cornwall: Portrait of a Society* (1941).

A. Hassell Smith, 'Justices at work in Elizabethan Norfolk', in *Norfolk Archaeology*, xxxiv, (1967), 93–110.

W. B. Willcox, *Gloucestershire: a Study in Local Government, 1590–1640* (New Haven, 1940).

IV

The County Community at War

D. H. PENNINGTON

In 1642, when the dispute between Charles I's supporters and a majority of the Commons, led by John Pym, came slowly to the point of armed conflict, the most conspicuous immediate effect was not the fighting but the breakdown of most of the old institutions of government. The king and his high officers of state left London, and the great seal that ratified every act of sovereignty went with them. Eventually a new Royalist capital was established at Oxford, where, briefly, a parliament of sorts met. At Westminster the remaining peers and M.P.s continued their proceedings with as little apparent change as possible. Since each half of the old machine controlled roughly half the country, each of them faced the same need to improvise a complete working government. Obviously it would have far more to do than before. Neither side could recruit, feed, equip, and pay large armies, fortify towns, hold the obedience of a bewildered population merely through the efforts of such of the J.P.s, undersheriffs, deputy lieutenants, and other existing officials as were prepared to help. Many more people would have to be involved in the governing work that had previously been the monopoly of a small section of the community. In this task of greater organization, parliament in the long run was more successful than the king. To see how this contributed to their victory would of course require a detailed comparative study of the two sides which has not yet been undertaken. The most we can do here is to look at the efforts of parliament. They are a good deal better recorded than those of the Royalists; and it was on the parliamentary side that general political and social questions were more deeply involved in the administrative improvisations.

As soon as the parliamentary opposition began to admit the possibility of making war on the royal government, they had to devise ways of getting control of men and money. This involved some awkward explanations. They still insisted that they were not attacking the king's supreme place in government: they merely claimed that he should exercise his power in and with parliament. They would not dream of calling for men to rise in rebellion; but it was necessary to take the existing local forces, the county militia, out of the hands of those who adhered to the king's 'evil counsellors'. Provisions for doing this were laid down in the 'Militia Bill' to which Charles would not, in any form acceptable to parliament, give the royal assent. The two houses had to issue it themselves in the form of an 'Ordinance of Parliament' which, on the strength of transparently bogus precedents, they claimed had legal validity.

> Whereas there hath been of late a most dangerous and desperate design upon the House of Commons which we have just cause to believe to be an effect of the bloody counsels of papists and other ill-affected persons, who have already raised a rebellion in the kingdom of Ireland, and we cannot but fear they will proceed to stir up the like insurrections in England; in this time of imminent danger it is ordained by the Lords and Commons now in Parliament assembled that. . . .

A lieutenant is named for each county, and each town that ranked as a county, in England and Wales, though as some held more than one such office there are only thirty-six names in all.

> They shall have power to assemble and call together all and singular His Majesty's subjects that are fit for the wars, to train exercise and put them in readiness, to nominate such persons of quality as to them seem meet to be their Deputy Lieutenants to be approved of by both Houses . . . and such persons shall answer their neglect and contempt to the Lords and Commons in a Parliamentary way and not otherwise.[1]

The lieutenancy was a familiar and respectable institution, usually

[1] *Acts and Ordinances of the Interregnum,* ed. C. H. Firth and R. S. Rait (1911), i. 1–5.

with one of the greatest peers of the region at its head and substantial county gentry as his deputies who did the real work of organizing the militia—not normally an arduous task. The old ruling families were thus to be the basis of parliament's military government. The king in raising forces made more use of a device that depended directly on his personal authority, the commission of array. The commissioners too were usually county gentry. In Cheshire, people spoke of the rival parties as 'they of the militia' and 'they of the array'; and Cheshire was one of the places where the two were so much alike that they soon made a private pact of neutrality. The allegiance of many areas depended simply on which side proved quicker and more effective in recruiting.

The next problem was money; and here too principles that had sounded so noble only a few months before became embarrassing. The Commons, having complained bitterly about the illegality of taxation without parliamentary consent, had to admit that taxation without royal consent was no less contrary to their notion of the constitution. Merchants were invited to go on paying their tonnage and poundage 'by way of loan', and appeals were sent out to every accessible part of the country for voluntary subscriptions of plate and money. But for the first winter of the war a great many counties did not send as much to London as they received from it. The enterprising provincial merchants or younger sons who had sought wealth in the capital and settled there suddenly became men of great importance to the parliamentary cause. With or without pressure from their counties, they came together to organize the sending home of urgently needed money, munitions, or even men. In February 1643 Warwickshire and Staffordshire sent simultaneous delegations to London to confer with the exiles from their counties who had already formed committees to raise funds in the City. Muskets, powder, bullets, and later a few pieces of artillery were bought and sent north. It was of course on a small scale compared with the activity of the London merchants in providing both the loans on which the central war effort depended and the financial institutions that replaced the exchequer. Guildhall became the parliamentary treasury, and the halls of city companies the headquarters of parliamentary committees that handled the various sources of revenue. But borrowing and old-style taxation could not solve the problem: a long war could only be paid for by taking a larger part of the wealth of the whole community than any government had demanded before. To do this required the continued exertions of an effective authority in every county and every parish under parliamentary control. In the spring of 1643, with few scruples about either constitutional legality or sanctity of property, parliament issued four long ordinances that created an entirely new fiscal system. They provided for a levy, the 'Weekly Pay', on everyone above the level of wage-labourer (with a provision, easier to enact than to enforce, for sharing the burden between landlord and tenant); for forced loans from all substantial property-owners; for the sequestration of Royalist estates; and for an excise. The last of these, and the most hated, was administered directly by the merchant community through a great number of local commissioners. The other three were to be managed by committees in every county, duly nominated in the ordinances.

This was part of the origin of the new county government. But in every county where parliament had a reasonably secure foothold there was a committee in being already. Sometimes no-one had really established it: it had begun simply as the deputy-lieutenants, who from meeting regularly and receiving a succession of parliamentary instructions that expanded their duties gradually became a permanent committee. In Kent instructions were addressed first to the 'deputy lieutenants and committees'—meaning men to whom a task was committed—then to 'the committees' and finally to 'the Committee of Kent'. More often parliament produced a list of men they charged to act with the deputy lieutenants and with the Earl of Essex or one of the commanders under him, to raise forces for defending the country and gradually for a wide variety of administrative and quasi-judicial functions. The instructions for Cheshire were typical of the early ones:

> You shall have power and authority to arm, train, and put in readiness all and every the inhabitants of that county fit for war, as well Trained Band as other volunteers . . . and the sheriffs and all other officers are hereby enjoined to assist you. . . . You shall oppose and suppress all rebellion and commotion within

the said County of Chester or in any other counties in association
with the said county. . . . You shall fight with and slay all such
as shall by force oppose you. . . . You shall defend and protect
His Majesty's good subjects from violence and oppression by the
illegal Commission of Array. . . . You shall or may call together
the inhabitants of the said county and propound to them what
horse, men, and arms they will find and maintain, and what
money, plate, horse, or victuals they will give, lend, or advance. . . . You shall or may . . . make and appoint such
colonels, captains, and other officers as shall be requisite. . . .[2]

How the functions of the committee developed depended partly
on what older institutions survived the disruption of the war. In
some counties, such as Sussex, quarter sessions continued with little
of their work related immediately to wartime upheavals. In others
justices, sometimes Royalists in a parliamentary area, ceased to do
much. Some committees consisted mainly of the knights and esquires
already dominant in local government; others were unfamiliar and
suspect from the beginning. The lists of names approved by parliament, and presumably supplied mainly by local M.P.s, often included
a few who turned out to be Royalists or neutrals, and others so garbled
as to be unrecognizable. Though the 'county committee' or 'militia
committee' was supposed to be different from those named in the
finance ordinances, in practice the membership was much the same.
There was little point in distinguishing between bodies so closely
related: they tended to become simply 'the committee'. Naturally
they were not the most popular of men. Cleveland, the royalist
poet, was eloquent about them:

A Committee man is the relics of regal government, but like
the holy relics he outbulks the substance whereof he is a remnant. . . . He is in the inquisition of the purse an authentic Gypsy,
that nips your bung with a canting Ordinance. . . . He is the
universal tribunal, for since these times all lawsuits fall to his
cognizance as in a great infection all diseases turn oft to the plague.
It concerns our masters the Parliament to look about them: if he
proceedeth at this rate the jack may soon come to swallow the

[2] *Civil War Tracts*, ed. J. A. Atkinson (Chetham Soc., n.s.65, 1909), pp.7–12.

pike. . . . Take a state-martyr, one that for his good behaviour hath paid the excise of his ears and so suffered capitivity for the land-piracy of ship-money; next a primitive freeholder, one that hates the king because he is a gentleman. Add to these a mortified bankrupt that helps out his false weights with some scruples of conscience, a new blue-stockinged justice lately made of a good basket-hilted yeoman, together with two or three equivocal sirs whose religion like their gentility is the extract of their acres. These are the simples of this precious compound, a kind of Dutch hotch-potch.[3]

The county committees were not much more admired by the central authorities than they were by the people under their care. The Committee of Both Kingdoms, struggling to establish some sort of general strategic control over the war, regarded them as the most benighted devotees of localism, interested only in furthering the particular interests of their county or of a faction within it. Letters poured from Derby House pleading with the counties to make their forces and funds available for the main war effort, appeasing their indignation at being neglected by the great armies and left to the mercy of the enemy, sorting out their petty grievances against the generals and against each other. The difficulty was that at this stage the use or even the threat of force against any dis-loyalty short of actually supporting the enemy was out of the question. The Northamptonshire committee was ordered to seek out and punish those of its soldiers who had deserted and returned home—a task far too costly to be worth while; the Herefordshire committee sent a formal petition to have one of its regiments dis-banded, and was fobbed off with a promise that they would soon be employed for the benefit of the county. The Committee of Kent set out the arguments that were expressed less frankly and less eloquently by many of the others:

Intelligence [comes] from all parts that the enemy are resolved to enter Kent, though to their utter destruction. We confess we desire not to purchase their ruin at so dear a rate. To be insensible of our own danger upon our frequent intelligence would argue

[3] J. Cleveland, *The Character of a Country Committee Man* (1649).

improvidence and stupidity; while to seem too sensible of any threatening ruin compared with the lingering destruction of the whole kingdom . . . would argue too much timidity. . . . But my lords, the case of our county differs from all others, for what we do and have done at most excessive charge is all out of our own purses. Nothing has been required of us as well to defend others as ourselves that hath not been cheerfully undergone. . . . We repent not of any service to the public, yet we must be accountable to our county. . . . To send out forces from our own defence . . . will argue so much improvidence as we shall lose all credit with our county and so be incapable of doing that service for the public we formerly have done.[4]

Though it was generally assumed in the seventeenth century that the county was the natural unit of local organization, the parliamentary leaders never imagined that it was the best unit for fighting a war. They tried hard to get counties to 'associate' for mutual defence, and their efforts led to a subdued conflict, (which has re-emerged from time to time ever since), between the traditional 'county' system and the artificial 'regional' one. On paper almost the whole country was divided among the associations, and county committees remembered their existence quite often when they wanted help from their neighbours. But it was only the Eastern Association that had a regular committee of its own and a central treasury. The men who directed from Cambridge the affairs of the Association became as jealous of their authority and autonomy as the counties within it were of theirs. They complained to the House of Commons both that too little of the money raised in the Association was allocated in the ordinances for its own defence and that the counties kept too much of it themselves instead of sending it to Cambridge. In 1645 they were indignant at the proposal to incorporate the army of the Association into the New Model Army. Indeed, it was partly because the forces of the Association under Manchester had become a highly successful military unit that the seven eastern counties were a more effective group than existed anywhere else. An ordinance of parliament 'associating' Stafford-

4 *Calendar of State Papers Domestic, 1644*, pp. 147–8.

shire, Warwickshire, and Shropshire was bound to be limited in its significance when the commander who had most authority in Staffordshire was Brereton from Cheshire, and Warwickshire relied on the Earl of Denbigh who also dominated Worcestershire.

On the whole the 'defence of the county' became less important as the war went on. It was the great armies, with colonels and generals contesting for power at the centre, that offered a prospect of victory; and when they were in the neighbourhood the committees looked pretty helpless. Armies demanded supplies, not only of money but of food, quarters, horses, everything down to the dung that provided the basic ingredient of gunpowder. County committees could make the collection of all these things a little more of a legal and equitable process and less like outright robbery. In doing so they imposed vastly increased duties on both old officials and the new ones they created. Round the harassed county treasurers there developed an assortment of functionaries such as the 'solicitors for sequestrations' or 'sequestration commissioners' who handled the complex process of seizing and managing or letting Royalist estates, the various 'commissaries' who dealt with corn, hay, timber, ammunition and so on, the 'high collectors' who sometimes shared the taxation work in the divisions or hundreds. But it was the wretched man at the bottom of the pyramid, the parish constable, who bore the worst of the burden. He had an uneviable job in peace time, when it involved only the presentation of offenders against local laws and perhaps the collection of a few rates and taxes. Now, suddenly, he was expected to bring in and account for, often from house-holders already impoverished by the immediate demands of soldiers, far bigger sums than most of them had ever been called on to pay. Everyone complained of his incompetence.

The distribution of the county's resources, in money and in kind, raised problems even more difficult politically than the collection of them. Parliament had started with the idea that all the money from the big taxes was to be sent to the capital and thence to the armies. But the slowness and danger of getting to London money that was needed locally gave the county authorities a good excuse for ignoring such orders. The treasurers, with or without parliamentary permission, kept a large part of what they got. It was a bitter blow to them when parliament introduced the compounding process by which Royalists could retrieve their estates for a lump sum paid in London, depriving the county of the revenue from sequestration. There remained the task of distributing money from the county treasuries among the military commanders great and small. Often the best that could be done was to link collecting and spending in a way that gave formal recognition to what tended to happen without it: funds from a particular area were allocated to a colonel, or even a captain, whose soldiers then helped the constables to extract it from the householders. The line between this and outright plunder could be a hazy one. Sometimes a commander was able to out-manoeuvre the committee by presenting an order from the Commons granting him the Weekly Pay or a special tax from a group of profitable parishes or even from a whole division of the county.

It was this financial chaos that led in 1644 to an attempt at administrative improvement that turned out to have far-reaching political consequences. After many abortive attempts to keep track of the money spent, parliament set up the Committee for Taking the Accounts of the Kingdom, under the chairmanship of the busiest of all its supporters, William Prynne. It began its work by setting up county committees of its own; and the general rule was laid down that their members must not belong to existing county committees of any kind. It followed that they had to consist of men who, for whatever reason, were not so far taking part in county government; and they became the centre of a tangle of quarrels that in many places seemed to matter more than winning the war against the Royalists. But there is a pattern in the tangle; and as evidence from more and more counties comes to light the similarity appears very striking. Parliament's original assumption was that the old ruling families in each county would run the new machinery as they had the old. How far this happened depended on local politics: both leading and lesser gentry could hold opinions that spread over a wide range to the left and right of the neutrality that at first a great many of them hoped to preserve. But the unprecedented tasks and institutions were an opportunity for new, active, zealous people. As more men became needed in local government, the balance in the committees tended to shift towards the minor manorial families who normally took little part in county affairs, and to the townsmen, the local lawyers, the men who had risen from obscurity in the armies. Sir John Oglander in the Isle of Wight picked out the two great complaints of the established gentry—that the committees were outside the familiar ruling set-up of the county and that they were not composed entirely of the landowning class.

> We had here a thing called a committee, which overruled Deputy Lieutenants and also Justices of the Peace; and of this we have brave men: Ringwood of Newport the pedlar, Maynard the apothecary, Matthews the baker, Wavell and Legge farmers. . . . These ruled the whole island and did whatever they thought good in their own eyes.[5]

To some of these men the county community did not mean very much; some of them grew less and less afraid to upset the stability of propertied society; some combined extreme Puritanism with political radicalism; some were the unscrupulous rogues their enemies pretended they all were. The quarrelling took many different forms: in Warwickshire there was a highly involved struggle between the accounts committee and the county committee with two factions appearing in each; in Kent the triumph of the radicals on the committee helped to drive moderates to rebel with the Royalists in 1648; in Staffordshire a military coup led to a half-hearted purge of the committee. Everywhere the quarrelling tended to resolve itself into a split between two attitudes to the Civil War. On one side were those who wanted to fight as much as was necessary to arrive at an acceptable peace settlement, but to preserve the old forms of society intact. On the other were those eager to win the war, throw out the courtiers, the bishops, the inner circle that monopolized power at the centre and in the counties. Localism, compromise, and social conservatism opposed centralism, militancy, and revolutionary Puritanism. One of the most consistent claims in the propaganda of the conservative Parliamentarians was that the radicals were 'mean, petty fellows', a gang of unheard-of climbers motivated only by greed, jealousy, and ambition. In fact there were

[5] John Oglander, *A Royalist's Notebook,* ed. F. Bamford (1936), pp. 110–11.

plenty of both types on both sides; but there is little doubt that in general there were significantly more from the old ruling groups and the richer families on the side of peace than on the side of war, and more of the 'new men' among the militants and later Cromwellians. Indeed it seems likely that this social division within the parliamentary side, more apparent at the level of the county than of parliament, is more marked than the differences between roundhead and cavalier.

The political quarrels, and the contribution of the county organization to the parliamentary victory, are bound to seem the most significant themes. But the committees did not spend most of their time on either. For the ordinary men and women of the towns and villages the Civil War was the worst of the many calamities they had known. If they had any prospect at all of help from the men in power, the committee was a possible source. Their daily routine represented a constant struggle to offer some haphazard justice and relief to a community where war had almost destroyed both the respect for law and order and the means of enforcing them. So far as orders on paper could do it, they remedied the worst sufferings: the man whose house had been destroyed was given a tree to build another; the woman robbed by soldiers was authorized to bring the thieves before the committee if she could; the poor were compensated for their worst losses by occasional small payments or such easy concessions as permission to gather firewood on Royalist estates; rough and ready arbitration was offered on some of the intricate disputes that arose from the upheaval in land tenure. Even the grievances of Royalist wives and families received leisurely consideration. On the whole it was power rather than patience that was lacking in the attempts to deal with endless individual misfortunes.

Whereas Mr. Abberley had eleven cows taken from him by the enemy it is ordered that he shall have two heifers and a white cow remaining in the committee's hands and one other which was taken away yesternight, if she can be found, if the right owner of the cow have not the same.[6]

[6] *The Committee at Stafford, 1643–5*, ed. D. H. Pennington and I. A. Roots (1957), p. 182.

It is well to remember from time to time that Mr. Abberley's cows mattered a great deal more to Mr. Abberley than the fate of King Charles I.

Books for further reading

M. Coate, *Cornwall in the Great Civil War* (2nd edn., 1963).

A. H. Dodd, *Studies in Stuart Wales* (1953).

A. M. Everitt, *The Community of Kent and the Great Rebellion, 1640–60* (1966).

Lotte Glow, 'The Committee of Safety', in *English Historical Review*, 80 (1965), 289–313.

P. Hardacre, *The Royalists in the Puritan Revolution* (The Hague, 1956).

E. Hughes, *Studies in Administration and Finance* (1934, chapter 4).

C. H. Mayo (ed.), *The Minutes of the Dorset Standing Committee* (1902).

V. Pearl, *London and the Outbreak of the Puritan Revolution* (1961).

C. V. Wedgwood, *The Common Man and the Civil War* (1958).

A. C. Wood, *Nottinghamshire in the Civil War* (1937).

V

The Growth of London

F. J. FISHER

Since it is the current fashion among historians to dress up their guesses with statistics, perhaps this essay too had better start with some figures. We do not know the exact population of London in the early seventeenth century. A census of 1631, it is true, showed 130,000 residents in the City proper, but that census might be unreliable, and, in any case, by this time men already talked and thought of a greater London, a London that stretched westward as far as Long Acre and Westminster, that included Clerkenwell in the north and Southwark across the river, that pushed long fingers of ribbon development along the roads to Shoreditch, to Bethnal Green, to Limehouse, to Rotherhithe and to Bermondsey. By the time of the Civil War the population of this area may have reached a quarter of a million. Already one Englishman in twenty may have been a Londoner.

By contrast, it is doubtful whether any provincial city had more than 20,000 inhabitants, and reasonably certain that only four or five had as many as 10,000. Thus, London differed from other towns not so much in degree as in kind. It was unique by virtue of its size as well as by virtue of its wealth. And to many historians that simple fact alone helps to explain much of what happened under the early Stuarts. They have observed the impact on English agriculture of the City's demand for food and the impact on English mining of its demand for fuel. They have rejoiced at the good fortune whereby London was able to maintain a commercial theatre when Shakespeare and his fellows were available to write for it.

But before going further with an attempt to consider the possible relations between what contemporaries thought of as this monstrous growth and the social tensions of the time, it is well to begin with a word of warning. It is important to remember that civil war is apt to produce situations and to breed emotions that the historian cannot safely read back into the pre-war period. Early in the Civil War, when the membership of both Lords and Commons was split, and before Cromwell's New Model Army had come into being, it was tempting to see the conflict very largely as one of London against the crown and the provinces. Thus it is easy to understand how a parliamentary pamphleteer could attempt to inspire enthusiasm by telling of the cavalier's prejudice against the City, how they had already shared the various properties out amongst themselves and resolved to murder their creditors 'so they say, "We shall be both out of debt and have money to boot." ' And it is equally easy to see that a Royalist could declare:

> If [posterity] shall ask who would have pulled the crown from the King's head, taken the government off the hinges, dissolved Monarchy, enslaved the laws, and ruined their country; say, twas the proud, unthankful, schismatical, rebellious, bloody City of London.[1]

But the pre-war evidence shows a much less melodramatic state of affairs. Although it is true that provincial merchants complained of the arrogance and success of their London competitors, and the provincial preachers thought of Londoners as peculiarly addicted to sin, in general the links between the capital and the country were close and their relationships were both amicable and mutually profitable. And although both James and Charles tried to check the growth of London, in this they were only continuing a policy that Elizabeth had begun at the request of the Lord Mayor and aldermen.

In fact, if social conflict means anything more than the tension and friction to be found in all human communities, it is difficult to find signs of it in early Stuart London. But of normal tension and friction there was plenty, for these are the accompaniments of change, and the growth of London was perhaps the greatest change

---

[1] *Somers Tracts* (1810), iv. 598.

that was happening at this time. Since London was the largest of English towns, it threw up on a large scale the social difficulties that elsewhere were still only just visible. And since it was the only really large town, it created problems peculiar to itself. Let us take those two categories in turn.

Any seventeenth-century corporate town, including the City of London itself, can crudely but conveniently be thought of as being divided into three social groups. At the bottom of the pyramid was the mass of wage-earners who provided the physical labour that an unmechanized community required. They were generally poor, and for the most part unskilled, and even those who had learned a trade were forbidden to practise it since they had not been admitted into the freedom of the town. Above them was a thinner layer of tradesmen and skilled artisans who, as free citizens, were entitled to set up business on their own, but whose scale of operations was usually extremely modest. And at the top was a small elite of wealthier business and professional men who monopolized the civic government.

In any town constructed in this way, there were three issues which could create a ferment. The first was the need to prevent the number of the labouring poor from exceeding the local demand for their labour. The larger the town the more difficult this was; and in the case of London the problem reached crisis dimensions. For the capital was the obvious Mecca for the ambitious and the footloose; it was the obvious market in which the out-of-work labourer could hope to get casual employment; it was by far the most promising milieu for the thief, the prostitute and the professional beggar. Moreover, as contemporaries complained, the influx of these people was encouraged by some London property-owners.

> The desire of Profit greatly increaseth Buildings and so much the more for that this great concourse of all sorts of people drawing near unto the City, every man seeketh out places, highways, lanes and covert corners to build upon, if it be but sheds, cottages and small tenements for people to lodge in, which have not any means either to live or to employ themselves about any other manner of thing, than either to beg, or steal, by which

means of idleness it comes to pass that in some one parish there are above two thousand people which do live without any man's knowledge how, not using any manner of art or trade. This sort of covetous builders exact greater rents, and do daily increase them, insomuch that a poor handicraftsman is not able by his painful labour to pay the rent of a small tenement and feed his family. These builders neither regard the good of the common-wealth, the preservation of the health of the City, the main-tenance of honest tradesmen, neither do they regard of what base condition soever their tenants are, or what lewd and wicked practices soever they use so as their exacted rents be duly paid, the which for the most part they receive either weekly or monthly.[2]

And while some created slums in this way by throwing up flimsy cottages for letting at inflated rents to immigrants, others did so by converting barns and stables into dwellings or by subdividing large but decayed houses into a multiplicity of tenements. So from the fifteen-eighties onwards the City authorities had repeatedly pointed out the dangers of the situation. A particularly detailed account of them is set out in a privy council order of 1632.

This day was read again the petition presented by the Lord Mayor, Aldermen and Commons of the City of London in which they remonstrate that the freedom of London which was here-tofore of very great esteem is grown to be of little worth by reason of the extraordinary enlargement of the suburbs where great numbers of trades and handicraftsmen do enjoy without charge equal benefit with the freemen of the City of London. And that the city on every side is much pestered with great multitudes of newly erected tenements which of late times have been and now are in building which daily draw multitudes of people especially of the meaner sort and many loose persons . . . and by occasion of these new erected buildings the markets in London are forestalled and the prices of all victuals raised, the pipes that convey water to the citizens are built upon, and it is not to be doubted that from these new buildings when the streets

[2] Quoted in N. G. Brett-James, *The Growth of Stuart London* (1936), pp. 98-9.

shall be paved much gravel, sand and soil will be conveyed into the river and navigation both eastwards and westwards thereby prejudiced. And likewise an apparent danger may grow to the City and suburbs in case of infection in regards that the City is encompassed with new erected tenements, the suburbs being now grown far bigger than the city.[3]

Consequently, from 1580 onwards there was a long stream of royal proclamations on the matter. These forbade the subdividing of old houses into tenements, and the erection of new dwellings without licence. They laid down specifications to which builders were to conform, and they established what a later generation would have called a Green Belt around the City. It is obvious that such measures did not stop the growth of London's population, and in so far as they discouraged building they may well have intensified those problems of overcrowding, high rents and public health that they were designed to solve.

And at the other end of the social scale, the mere size of London also made serious a tension that was comparatively unimportant elsewhere. Traditionally, the urban artisan producing consumer goods for a local market, sold direct to his customers without the aid of any middleman, and in most provincial towns this was still the normal procedure. But in some of London's more fashionable trades the functions of the retailer were becoming separated from those of the actual producer. This was not surprising in itself. Not only do large markets normally encourage specialization and the division of labour, but in a large city there are good reasons why retailing should be concentrated along the main thoroughfares while actual production is carried on in the back streets or even in the suburbs. Yet the separation inevitably led to fears that the few and relatively wealthy shopkeepers would exploit the more numerous and much poorer artisans. And when those artisans came to depend for the supply of their raw materials on the same shopkeepers that distributed their products, their fears were increased. And the agitation of the small London master craftsman against the growing subjection to capitalist middlemen is one of the most prominent themes of

[3] Public Record Office, Privy Council Register, 29 Nov., 1632.

London history under the early Stuarts. A typical expression of his views can be found in the complaints of the leather-dressers (the glovers, pointmakers and white tawyers) against the leather-sellers.

> For whereas in all other trades, though the shopkeepers grow-ing rich do make the workmen their underlings, yet they suffer them according to their increase of ability to become like them-selves, and in the meantime to exercise the favour and privilege of their company and society; and though in some trades the shopkeepers sell to the workmen their materials, yet they take them again from them wrought and manufactured at reasonable rates, as Goldsmiths, Skinners, Silkmen and divers others. But the Leathersellers who pretend themselves to be of the same trade with the Glovers, Pointmakers and White Tawyers if they once put their griping hands betwixt the Grower or the Merchant and any of the said Trades they never part with the commodities they buy till they sell them at their own pitched rates without either regard or care whether the workmen be able to make his money thereof or no.[4]

The traditional instrument for the protection of an artisan's interest was, of course, his gild. But by the early seventeenth cen-tury the control of virtually every City gild had passed out of the hands of its artisan members. As a result, the early Stuarts received a long series of demands, either for the reform of the existing gilds or for the separate organization of the artisans. And, in fact, new gilds of small masters were numerous and were found, for example, among the felt-makers, the glovers, the skinners, the pinmakers and many others. But organization by itself solved little, for the bargain-ing power of the shopkeepers and middlemen still remained pre-dominant. Hence some of these gilds developed what may be thought of as a bastard form of co-operation. A common fund was set up for the purchase of raw materials and for the repurchase of finished products from members. But since the members of the gild were poor, the necessary capital had to be obtained from outside. The Pinmakers Company, for example, got their finance from the

[4] Quoted in G. Unwin, *Industrial Organization in the Sixteenth and Seven-teenth Centuries* (1904), p. 129.

government for they were able to negotiate a contract with the king. Usually, however, a new gild could only get its stock or capital from a private capitalist—and often from the very same man who had been instrumental in getting them a charter—and thus the artisans bound themselves to a single monopolist in place of the hated shopkeepers. Their last stage was seldom more prosperous than the first, and this struggle of the artisans against control by men wealthier than themselves is perhaps the nearest approach to a real social conflict that seventeenth century London could show.

But from the point of view of the Lord Mayor and aldermen another issue was more immediately important. They, like the magistrates of every other corporate town, were concerned to maintain the value of the City's privileges by restricting production and distribution to those who had been admitted to the City's freedom. Yet, even more than the magistrates of provincial towns, they found that policy difficult to enforce. It was not easy to suppress interlopers in the crowded wards of the City. If suppressed in the City, they easily moved into the prosperous suburbs, where the City had no jurisdiction. When Charles offered to extend the City's jurisdiction over the suburbs the Lord Mayor and aldermen refused to add to their responsibilities. And when, as a result, Charles created a separate corporation for Westminster and the other suburbs, it looked as though the privileged position of London's citizens might well be eroded.

Despite the size of London, it would be possible to treat all these issues as simply matters of local history were it not for the fact that they were all in some measure tied to one of the main themes of the time—the crown's chronic lack of money. James and Charles no doubt banned the erection of new buildings in good faith, but they enforced the ban not by pulling down new buildings but by taxing those who erected them—a procedure that pleased neither the City authorities who had asked for their destruction, nor the builders who paid the taxes, nor the tenants who had to rent them. The new gilds of small masters may have been designed in the interests of their members, but they tended to work to the profit of the businessman who purchased a charter and privileges on their behalf. And the new corporation of Westminster and the suburbs was also expected to raise money for the crown. For those reasons, all these local issues got drawn into the general disagreement between king and parliament.

But of course there were developments in London to which there were really no provincial equivalents. The Tudor and Stuart monarchy depended for its stability partly on a strict censorship of the written word and the suppression of popular discussion about affairs of state. In the small communities of provincial England those restrictions were enforced with some success; but as London grew larger not all the powers of the Star Chamber could effectively quell the pamphleteering and the gossip of the capital. The Earl of Clarendon, reflecting upon the reigns of James I and Charles I put this point trenchantly.

> There cannot be a better instance of the unruly and mutinous spirit of the city of London, which was the sink of all the ill humour of the kingdom, than the triumphant entry which some persons at that time made into London, who had been before seen upon pillories, and stigmatized as libellous and infamous offenders; of which classis of men scarce any age can afford the like.[5]

Nor did those ill humours remain in that sink, for the gossip and rumours of London were circulated to the provincial gentry by assiduous letter writers and whispered in taverns by the carters and carriers who handled inland trade. Moreover, to the exciting political and social gossip of the taverns there were added the less exciting but potentially more dangerous sermons of the radical clergy. Londoners could afford the best preachers; Londoners got the best preachers; and most of the best preachers were Puritans.

Even more important was the fact that London owed its expansion partly to a change in the habits of the country gentry. Members of that class had long been visiting the capital on legal and other business. But in the early seventeenth century their visits seem to have become longer and more frequent, although it was still the custom for them to stay in hotels and lodgings rather than to

[5] Edward Hyde, Earl of Clarendon, *History of the Rebellion and Civil Wars* (1839), i. 323–4.

possess town houses of their own. Lawsuits were the curse of the age and few gentlemen could avoid them. London was the great market both for the purchase of land and for the negotiation of marriages. Above all, it was the one place in England that could offer real relief from the intolerable tedium of country life. And, with the increasing use of the coach, men no longer found it so easy to leave their wives at home. The enthusiasm with which their wives accompanied them led to James's famous and ungallant outburst against:

> Those swarms of gentry who, through the instigation of their wives and to new model and fashion their daughters (who, if they were unmarried marred their reputations, and if married lost them), neglect their country hospitality and are a burden to the city and a general nuisance to the kingdom.[6]

For the matter was serious. The essentially patriarchal system of Stuart England depended on the willingness of landlords to reside in the provinces where they could act both as employers and as representatives of the state. Landlords who spent much or all of their time in London served neither purpose. Nor was this all. When parliament was in abeyance, visits to London provided great opportunities for the opposition leaders to keep in touch with each other. And if the Venetian ambassador is to be trusted, Charles was both aware of those opportunities and alarmed by them. Consequently, it is not surprising to find that measures to prevent the growth of London in general were increasingly supplemented by others to discourage the gentry in particular. Some of those measures could be indirect, as one gossip-writer explained to his client.

> We have very plausible things done of late. To encourage Gentlemen to live more willingly in the country all Game Fowl— as Pheasants, Partridges, Ducks and Hares—are by proclamation forbidden to be dressed or eaten in any Inns, and Butchers forbidden to be Graziers.[7]

Normally, however, a more direct approach was preferred; the gentry were ordered out of town by proclamation and laggards

---

[6] I. Disraeli, *Curiosities of Literature* (1834), vi. 175.
[7] W. Knowler, *The Earl of Stafford's Letters and Dispatches* (1739), i. 176.

risked prosecution in the Star Chamber. How far provincial life
benefited we don't know; but it can hardly have pleased either the
gentry who were treated like schoolboys or the London catering and
entertaining industries that depended on their custom.

Finally, it must not be forgotten that London was the financial
centre of the economy and that the Stuarts were dependent on the
City for loans in a twofold sense—they depended on the citizens to
provide the money and on the Lord Mayors and aldermen to collect
that money for them, since no banking system yet existed. His ability
to borrow from the City had enabled James to dispense with
Parliament for nearly ten years. It was Charles' inability to continue
borrowing that forced him to call Parliament in 1640. And under
James, Londoners had not only lent generously to the crown but
they had largely financed the settlement of Ireland on the crown's
behalf. One of the major mistakes of the Stuarts was to destroy their
credit with the City. And this is how Clarendon put the matter: as
London was rich

> . . . it was looked upon too much of late time as a com-
> mon stock not easy to be exhausted, and as a body not to be
> grieved by ordinary acts of injustice; and therefore it was not
> only a resort, in all cases of necessity, for the sudden borrowing
> great sums of money . . . but it was thought reasonable, upon
> any specious pretences, to revoke the security that was at any
> time given for money so borrowed. So . . . a grant made by
> the King in the beginning of his reign (in consideration of great
> sums of money) of good quantities of land in Ireland and the city
> of Londonderry there, was avoided by a suit in the star chamber;
> all the lands, after a vast expense in building and planting, re-
> sumed into the king's hands, and a fine of fifty thousand pounds
> imposed upon the city. Which sentence . . . made a general im-
> pression in the minds of the citizens of all conditions, much to
> the disadvantage of the court; and though the king afterwards
> remitted to them the benefit of that sentence, they imputed that
> to the power of the parliament, and rather remembered how it
> had been taken from them, than by whom it was restored.[8]

[8] Clarendon, ii. 142–3.

Thus, if no great social conflicts appear in the history of London at this time, there was plenty of friction. And that friction was important. As I see it, the famous Civil War was the result less of a major social conflict than of the break-down of a clumsy political machine in the hands of a remarkably inefficient operator. But the difficulties of Charles I were increased by changes that were making England more difficult to govern, and the growth of London was among the most important of those changes. And when the machine did break down the influence of London was vital. It was fear of the London crowd that on occasion drove the House of Lords to agree with the House of Commons; it was the City authorities who protected the five members of the Commons whom Charles tried to arrest for treason. And it was the City militia that prevented Charles from opening the war with a knockout blow. That was why some were to attribute all the political evils of the time to London.

Books for further reading

N. G. Brett-James, *The Growth of Stuart London* (1936).

F. J. Fisher, 'The development of the London food-market', and 'The development of London as a centre of conspicuous consumption', in *Essays in Economic History*, ed. E. M. Carus-Wilson, i (1954), ii (1962).

V. Pearl, *London and the Outbreak of the Puritan Revolution* (1961).

VI

Puritanism, Politics and Society

AUSTIN WOOLRYCH

Puritans are elusive people in early Stuart England, and the first problem is to identify them. It is not that they are self-effacing—far from it. The difficulty is to draw any firm line between Puritans and the rest of protestant Englishmen. It is really a mistake to try, for the majority of them were in no sense a sect apart. We can best think of 'Puritan' and 'Anglican' as rough terms for describing two polarities within the broad national church which had taken shape under Queen Elizabeth. Between the two poles there was room for many shades of opinion, and in seeking to characterize them we must think in terms of differences of emphasis, not of two opposed faiths.

We must begin with matters of faith and worship and discipline, for these were what Puritanism was really about. The Puritan emphasis was on the tremendous responsibility of the individual conscience rather than on outward observance and institutional religion. Puritan divines in the early seventeenth century were taking some of the harsh rigour out of Calvin's doctrine of predestination, but they still dwelt on the gulf which lay between the elect, who by the free gift of God's grace gained assurance of salvation, and the reprobate, who were foredoomed to perdition. They conceived of themselves as a ministry dedicated to preaching the Word of God, rather than as a priesthood whose prime function was to celebrate the sacraments. They preached in order to awaken each individual soul to its peril, to make it receptive to grace by a conviction of sin, and then to guide it through the throes of spiritual rebirth. They preached also to direct the conscience on thorny problems of morality, for only by their conduct could the elect be truly known, even to themselves: 'by their fruits ye shall know them.' They all in their different ways pursued the ideal of a godly community on earth, and this involved the necessity of a spiritual jurisdiction over the faithful. The quest for a 'godly discipline' is one of the most persistent Puritan characteristics.

For Puritans, the Bible was the sole infallible guide to faith, worship and conduct; they acknowledged no parallel authority in the tradition of the church. They scrupled at Anglican ceremonies that had no scriptural warrant, and they rejected the Anglican claim that there was a wide field of 'things indifferent', meaning matters of church government and other outward forms that the state might regulate since the Bible did not pronounce on them. For the Puritans it was all there in the Book. They wanted to see the English church aligned with the reformed churches of the continent; in their enmity to Rome they were far more uncompromising than the High Anglicans, and the more radical of them identified the papacy with Antichrist.

These attitudes which Puritans held in common were more important than the differences which came to divide them. Until the Civil War the great majority of them were still comprehended within the national church. A few little break-away congregations of sectaries or separatists constituted only a minor exception as yet. There had been attempts under Elizabeth to graft a Presbyterian organization and discipline upon the Church of England, but these had been firmly repressed by Whitgift and Bancroft, and Presbyterianism was not much heard of again in England before the Great Rebellion broke out. Independency or congregationalism, which asserted a limited right for each congregation to order its own discipline and worship, was making more headway by the sixteen-thirties, but even those Independents who headed the great migration to New England did not renounce communion with the Church of England. And Independents were still a small minority among Puritans.

Although my main concern is with the political and social attitudes of Puritans, I have begun by sketching their strictly religious convictions in order to put first things first. There has been tremendous discussion of the thesis—not often advanced so confidently nowadays as it once was—that Puritanism was essentially the religion of an urban middle class, a version of Christianity moulded to accommodate the business practices of merchant capitalists. Marxists have seen it as the ideology of the bourgeoisie. I cannot point out the pitfalls in this thesis here, nor would I dispute a certain psychological affinity between the austere religious individualism of the Puritan faith and the sober economic individualism of the mercantile classes. But Puritanism was not just a religion of townsmen, for it ramified through every order of society. It enjoyed wide support among the landed gentry, from affluent knights down to depressed squireens, and its converts were certainly not restricted to the minority of landowners who shared in the entrepreneurial activities of the merchants. At least a fifth of the peers were Puritan in 1640, and so, at the other end of the scale, were thousands of small craftsmen and workpeople who were not so much the exploiters of rising capitalism as its victims. The social range of Puritanism would gradually narrow after the Restoration, but until then we should beware of regarding it, let alone 'explaining' it, as the religion of any one social order.

Puritanism grew up within a hierarchical society, and most Puritans accepted its traditional values. Very many of their ministers came of gentry stock. They were educated mainly in Cambridge colleges, where social status was strongly demarcated, and their typical path to a parish living lay through the patronage of a Puritan squire or peer. Others found a pulpit through what were known as lectureships—regular preaching appointments which were generally paid for by the most substantial local citizens. Others again served as chaplains and tutors in the households of great Puritan landlords, who in this way maintained preachers to whom parish livings might be debarred. It came naturally to the Puritan clergy to preach social subordination, and they did so. Here is William Perkins, the greatest of them in late Elizabethan times:

> God hath appointed that in every society one person should be above or under another; not making all equal, as though the body should be all head and nothing else: but even in degree and order, he hath set a distinction, that one should be above another.[1]

[1] William Perkins, *The Workes* (1612–13), i. 755; quoted in C. H. and K. George, *The Protestant Mind of the English Reformation, 1750–1640* (Princeton, N.J., 1961), p. 92.

And here, a generation later, is Thomas Adams:

> If God gives to some men honour, it is then to manifest that God
> allows difference of persons. He ordains some to rule and others
> to obey . . . he setteth some up on high, and placeth others in a
> low degree. To repine at others' greatness and our own meanness,
> is to cavil with God. . . . It is a savage and popular humour, to
> malign and inveigh against men in eminent places. That rhyme,
> 'When Adam delved and Eve span: who was then a gentleman?'
> seems to be made among Jack Straw's followers, and to savour of
> rebellious discontent.[2]

Of course many a preacher did 'inveigh against men in eminent
places'. Here is one of them:

> Of all men under heaven, none had so much need to pray as
> courtiers. . . . They are set upon the hill, and see the glory of the
> kingdoms of the earth, but I fear it is seen of them . . . the more
> need, the less devotion.[3]

But this was no Puritan. This was Joseph Hall, preaching before
King James I himself. He subsequently became a bishop, wrote a
treatise on the divine right of episcopacy, and was impeached and
imprisoned by the Long Parliament. Puritans too attacked the vices
of the privileged, but they had no monopoly of social criticism, and
it was not often as virulent as Hall's. It was one thing to denounce
men of social or political power for abusing their responsibilities; it
was quite another to question their claim to deference and obedience.
This the Puritans rarely did; respect for degree and status was on the
whole common ground.

Social subordination was closely linked with political subordination, and here too the typical Puritan was far from being a revolutionary before the Civil War. It is true that Puritans were often in the
forefront of opposition to Stuart policies. In contemporary terms,
they tended to side with the Country against the Court. The reasons
are obvious: the whole tone of court life, the pro-Spanish foreign
policy during most of the period, the flourishing of popery in high

[2] Thomas Adams, *The Works* (1629), p. 872; quoted in George, p. 93.
[3] Joseph Hall, *The Works* (1628–62), iii. 173; quoted in George, pp. 248–9.

places, Charles I's fatal promotion of Arminian divines in both church and state, to name only a few. But again, Puritans had no monopoly in opposing such things; and again, it was the abuse of authority they attacked and not the system of authority itself.

Before the revolution they never faltered in upholding the obedience which subjects owed to kings by the law of God. There was scarcely a breath among them of the doctrine that justified resistance to a tyrant prince, such as the Huguenots had advanced during the French Wars of Religion, or George Buchanan in Scotland. On the contrary, they preached the divine right of kings. This is William Perkins:

> God therefore hath given to kings, and to their lawful deputies, power and authority not only to command and execute his own laws, commanded in His word: but also to ordain and enact other good and profitable laws of their own, for the more particular governments of their people. . . . And further, God hath given these gods upon earth, a power as to make these laws and annexe these punishments.[4]

In the sixteen-twenties, the equally Puritan Robert Bolton could declare:

> Sovereignty is sacred in itself; authority even abstracted, is orient and illustrious, a ray and representation of that great Majesty above.[5]

> Even a contemptuous thought of a king, or lawful authority, is a sin of high nature; and methinks . . . is paralleled in *Ecclesiastes*, to the bloodiness of actual murther.[6]

In the 'thirties John Downame and Thomas Gataker upheld divine right even more uncompromisingly.

There were of course elements in the Puritan faith that could and did embolden political opposition: the overriding claims of the individual conscience, the ultimate superiority of the spiritual aristocracy

[4] Perkins, *Works*, ii. 437; quoted in George, p. 216.
[5] Robert Bolton, *The Works* (1631-41), i. 4f.
[6] *Ibid.*, iv. 72-3; this and the previous quotation in George, p. 217.

of the elect over the worldly aristocracy of birth and estate, the pursuit of the godly community and the aspiration to realize the Kingdom of God. It is also true that the organizations which kept the chief leaders of opposition in mutual contact all through the years of Charles I's personal rule—the Providence Island Company and the Saybrook Company—were Puritan colonizing ventures. But before the Civil War the Puritans did not develop an ideology of revolt in any way comparable to that of the French Huguenots or the Scottish Presbyterians. Towards both monarchy and the social hierarchy they broadly maintained the Tudor tradition.

They were certainly not disposed to rebel for the sake of religion. There were remarkably few attacks on episcopacy as such between 1590 and 1641. Most Puritans, even under Archbishop Laud, would have been content if the bishops had been removed from parliament and council and reduced to the ecclesiastical status of their Elizabethan forebears. The prayer book was a bigger bone of contention, but the moderate majority would have been reasonably satisfied if a few objectionable ceremonies had been dispensed with. They were far more concerned to reverse what they considered to be the innovations introduced by Laud and the Arminians than to inaugurate a wholesale revision of the Elizabethan settlement. In the church, as in the state and society, they were more conservative than revolutionary. Even that arch-Puritan William Prynne contended only for a moderate, primitive episcopacy until he went over to the radicals in 1641.

In that year of acute tension, however, a party really did gather strength which aimed to abolish the whole ecclesiastical hierarchy, root and branch. It was encouraged by the example of Scotland and by the Long Parliament's striking achievements in constitutional reform. It was supported too by a more extreme and popular kind of Puritanism that had lately been gathering strength in London and other major towns, the Puritanism of the sects. These conventicles of craftsmen and small traders were banned by the law and obnoxious to sober, orthodox Puritans, but they nourished the radical ardours of the young John Lilburne and other future leaders of the Levellers. We should not however exaggerate their influence at this stage. According to that moderate Puritan divine, Richard Baxter,

The remnant of the old Separatists and Anabaptists in London was then very small and inconsiderable; but they were enough to stir up the younger and inexperienced sort of religious people to speak too vehemently and intemperately against the bishops and Church and ceremonies, and to jeer and deride at the Common Prayer and all that was against their minds.[7]

A bill to extirpate episcopacy 'root and branch' failed to pass the House of Commons in 1641. Even the Grand Remonstrance, which the Commons passed in November by a bare eleven votes, said nothing of abolishing bishops. A clause in it condemning the prayer book was voted down by the House. And it further declared

> that it is far from our purpose or desire to let loose the golden reins of discipline and government in the Church, to leave private persons or particular congregations to take up what form of Divine Service they please, for we hold it requisite that there should be throughout the whole realm a conformity to that order which the laws enjoin according to the Word of God.[8]

Religious issues would never of themselves have led to civil war. Admittedly the radicals intended to reform the national church by act of parliament, but if king and Commons could have come to terms over the militia and the nomination of officers of state they would assuredly have reached a compromise over church government and worship. Even Cromwell later acknowledged that 'religion was not the thing at the first contested for'.[9]

Yet though the issues before the nation on the eve of civil war were primarily political, religion powerfully affected the way people chose sides on them. Baxter put it fairly:

> But though it must be confessed that the public safety and liberty wrought very much with most, especially with the nobility and gentry who adhered to the parliament, yet it was principally the differences about religious matters that filled up the parliament's

[7] *Autobiography of Richard Baxter* (London, 1931; abridgement of *Reliquiae Baxterianae*, 1696), p. 29.

[8] *Constitutional Documents of the Puritan Revolution, 1625–60*, ed. S. R. Gardiner (3rd edn., 1606), p. 229.

[9] W. C. Abbott, *The Writings an Speeches of Oliver Cromwell*, (Cambridge, Mass., 1937–47), iii. 586.

armies and put the resolution and valour into their soldiers, which carried them on in another manner than mercenary soldiers are carried on. Not that the matter of bishops or no bishops was the main thing (for thousands that wished for good bishops were on the parliament's side). . . .[10]

As it turned out, the brutal facts of civil war settled 'the matter of bishops or no bishops'. Most of the Lords and many of the Commons left Westminster to join the king, and this left the root-and-branch men in command of parliament for the first time. The bishops themselves were solidly Royalist; their abolition became inevitable. The Puritan clergy rapidly raised their sights as the prospects opened of a more thorough reformation than they had dared to hope for, and the form it would take was determined when parliament called in the Scots as allies in 1643. The Scottish price for military aid was a Presbyterian Church of England.

Here was an undreamt of opportunity to remake the national church according to the strict Word of God. The Presbyterian model commended itself to the Assembly of Divines at Westminster, not only because of Scottish pressure and the long-sanctified example of other reformed churches, but because it offered the readiest means of imposing that 'godly discipline' for which they had hankered ever since Calvin first tyrannized Geneva. Parliament saw to it that the discipline was kept within bounds, and characteristically exempted the nobility from it. But parliament too saw virtues in Presbyterianism, besides its alleged foundation in the Word of God. Suitably modified, it seemed the best way of preserving an all-embracing national church, under parliament's ultimate authority instead of the crown's, while still keeping the effective patronage over parish livings mainly in the hands of the well-affected nobility and gentry.

The new church, however, soon showed itself more intolerant than the old. Its very rigidity widened the rifts that were already appearing in the Puritan ranks. It was established in the teeth of protests from the Independents, many of whom returned from exile. These men asked for no general toleration, and indeed their brethren in New England were proving far from tolerant. They simply

[10] *Autobiography of Richard Baxter*, p. 34.

wanted liberty to follow 'the congregational way'—to base their churches not on mere common habitation of a parish but on a mutual covenant between men and women who could give testimony of their regeneration. But both parliament and the Assembly of Divines were against them, and by 1645 their hopes depended on the New Model Army. The army however included not only Independents but many sectaries of a more radical kind, and Cromwell demanded liberty for them all. The outcome was that the Independents were driven, though with misgivings and qualifications, to make common cause with the sects for a general liberty of conscience.

These sects multiplied amazingly during and after the Civil War. Through the ferment of the times their preachers caught intoxicating glimpses of the New Jerusalem; they fired their flocks with an intense and questing enthusiasm which broke through the confines of sober Puritan orthodoxy at many a point. There was a strong vein of social radicalism in this sectarian fervour, reflecting the relatively humble social milieu in which it took root, and it flourished particularly in London and in the army. The sects demanded not only toleration but the total removal of religion from the state's authority, and in this they found an early champion in Roger Williams. Williams had emigrated to Massachusetts, but having found the bounds of orthodoxy there too narrow for his own radical religious community, he removed it to Rhode Island and returned to England to obtain a charter for his settlement. Here in 1644 he published *The Bloudy Tenent of Persecution*. The Long Parliament had it burnt by the common hangman, but its ideas were not to be silenced.

> The Church or company of worshippers (whether true or false) is like unto a body or college of physicians in a city; like unto a corporation, society or company of East-India or Turkey merchants, or any other society or company in London: which companies may hold their courts, keep their records, hold disputations; and in matters concerning their society, may dissent, divide, break into schisms and fractions . . . yea wholly break up and dissolve into pieces and nothing, and yet the peace of the city not be in the least measure impaired or disturbed; because

the essence of being of the city, and so the well-being and peace thereof is essentially distinct from those particular societies; the city-courts, city-laws, city punishments distinct from theirs.[11]

This may not sound startling today, but it broke on a world that had always regarded church and state as two aspects of one community, each equally all-embracing. The notion of opting out of the church seemed as subversive as declining to accept the kingdom's laws. Now the sects were saying that religion was none of the state's business; the civil magistrate had to do only with the natural man; all forcing of conscience was tyranny; churches were voluntary associations of believers, and government should no more interfere with their internal affairs than with those of a trading company or a professional organization.

Conservative opinion, including that of the Presbyterians, found this shocking on two counts. It was horrified at the idea of tolerating heresy, and it was convinced that a national church was a necessary bond of both government and society. What would happen if the state parted with the power to tune the pulpits? What social anarchy would not ensue if preachers were democratically elected by congregations of cobblers and the like, instead of being presented by gentry patrons or parliamentary committees? For under this English Presbyterianism the power of ordination vested in the presbyteries (whose elders anyway would normally be gentry-dominated) was complementary to the traditional rights of patrons and did not supplant them.

This consternation grew still stronger when the sort of folk whom the sects had helped to awaken into political consciousness were offered a very positive political programme by the Levellers. It was a largely secular programme* but the Levellers clearly sought to harness religious radicalism to political radicalism. John Lilburne, for instance, based his claim that all men were born to equal natural rights upon the assumption that God had bestowed sovereignty over all the rest of his creatures upon Adam and Eve, and that therefore none of their descendants had rightful power or authority over any others

[11] Quoted in P. Miller and T. H. Johnson, *The Puritans* (New York, 1963), i. 220.
* See below, chapter 10.

except by mutual consent. Moreover the Levellers sponsored the extreme sectarian claim that religion lay altogether outside the power entrusted to the civil magistrate.

The Levellers made many recruits among the sects. To the Presbyterians, and to parliament generally, their doctrines were anathema. The Independents were less uniformly hostile, but they were deeply suspicious of the concept of natural equality. In November 1647, just after the Putney Debates, a group of Independent churches in and about London published a declaration which contained this passage:

> And since every man is not alike qualified for the same action, nor hath that discretion and propension of his own accord to fall into that place which is most proper for him; and since also there is so much darkness remaining in the minds of men, as to make them subject to call evil good, and good evil; . . . it cannot but be very prejudicial to human society, and the promotion of the good, of commonwealths, cities, armies or families, to admit of a parity, or all to be equal in power. . . .
>
> And therefore we cannot but conclude, that the ranging of men into several and subordinate ranks and degrees, is a thing necessary for the common good of men, as being the only means to remove obstructions, and to preserve order.[12]

Orthodox Puritans could never pass over the Fall of Man as Lilburne did, for they held that man's judgement and will were so corrupted by Adam's sin that subordination was a political and social necessity. Even the support that the Levellers drew from the sects began to falter after a while. One strain in sectarian feeling could be channelled towards democracy, by segregating altogether the spheres of spiritual and secular authority, but another pointed in just the opposite direction. This other strain of radical Puritanism based its hopes not on a popular commonwealth but on the millennium—the literal advent of Christ's kingdom on earth. Far from setting aside the huge gulf between the elect and the reprobate, as the Levellers did, these millenarians asserted the claim of the elect—the saints, as they called

[12] *A Declaration by Congregational Societies in and about the City of London* (1647), p. 7.

themselves—to govern the rest of fallen mankind. A rule of the saints must be established now, to prepare for the imminent reign of Christ as king. Such a purpose was the antithesis of Leveller egalitarianism, and they knew it. They asked

> What right or claim mere natural and worldly men have to rule and government, that want [i.e. lack] a sanctified claim to the least outward blessings? How can the Kingdom be the saints' when the ungodly are electors, and elected to govern? We expect new heavens and a new earth, according to His promise. How then can it be lawful to patch up the old worldly government, especially being lapsed? How dangerous it is to keep Christ from His throne when He hath exalted you and given you an opportunity to exalt Him.[13]

The purging of the parliament, the execution of Charles I and the erection of the Commonwealth all marked the Independents' victory over the Presbyterians. The Levellers met their crucial defeat soon after, when their mutinies in the army were broken. From 1649, millenarian enthusiasm rose as the Leveller movement declined, and it gained a powerful following in the army. When the first great crisis of the Commonwealth culminated in 1653 with Cromwell's expulsion of the Rump, the fanatics who sought a rule of the saints thought their day had come. They made their bid for power in Barebone's Parliament, which was not an elected body at all but one hand-picked by the army officers. Cromwell showed how far he himself was touched by the millenarian spirit when he addressed it at its opening:

> I confess I never looked to see such a day as this. . . . Jesus Christ is owned this day by your call, and you own Him by your willingness to appear for Him; and you manifest this, as far as poor creatures can, to be the day of the power of Christ. . . . Why should we be afraid to say or think that this may be the door to usher in the things that God has promised, which have been prophesied of?[14]

13 *Certain Queries Presented by Many Christian People* (1649), printed in *Puritanism and Liberty*, ed. A. S. P. Woodhouse (1938), p. 246.
14 *The Writings and Speeches of Oliver Cromwell*, iii. 63–4.

But Cromwell was soon disillusioned. Barebone's Parliament taught him that the saints could be as subversive of social and political order as the Levellers. After five months he accepted its resignation with relief. At last he shouldered the burden of the headship of the state, as Lord Protector. It was time to bring 'the people of God' back to earth. For five more years all but the most fanatical of them accepted the shelter of his sword, for his broad established church was based on no one Puritan denomination, and the sectaries who could not conscientiously find a home within it were given the widest freedom of worship outside it. But even he could not teach his own tolerance either to the saints or to his parliaments.

By this time Puritanism had suffered as great a fragmentation as the parliamentary cause itself. Since so few could separate politics from religion, political divisions helped to harden religious schisms, and vice versa. The proliferation of New Jerusalems in the revolutionary years had broken the broad unity of pre-war Puritanism, even in matters of faith. From Elizabeth's reign to that of Charles I, the mission of Puritanism had been to revitalize the spiritual and moral life of the nation within the framework of a broadly comprehensive national church. Cromwell made the last attempt to erect such a comprehensive church; the makers of the Restoration settlement firmly turned their backs on it. They marked out the great divide between church and chapel, and for a whole generation they deepened it by persecution. From the Puritan point of view at least, what we used to call the Puritan Revolution ended in defeat.

Books for further reading

C. H. and K. George, *The Protestant Mind of the English Reformation, 1570–1640* (Princeton, N.J., 1961). Contrast their views with those of J. F. New, *Anglican and Puritan: the basis of their opposition* (1964).

W. Haller, *The Rise of Puritanism* (New York, 1938; Harper Torchbooks paperback).

W. Haller, *Liberty and Reformation in the Puritan Revolution* (New York, 1955; Columbia paperback).

J. E. C. Hill, *Society and Puritanism* (1964).

J. E. C. Hill, *Puritanism and Revolution* (1958; Mercury paperback): ch. 1, 7 and 8.

W. K. Jordan, *The Development of Religious Toleration in England, 1558–1660*, 4 vols. (1932–40). Vols. iii and iv deal with the period 1640–60.

W. M. Lamont, *Marginal Prynne* (1963).

Perry Miller, *The New England Mind* (New York, 1939), esp. ch. 1–3.

G. Nuttall, *Visible Saints* (1957).

W. A. Shaw, *A History of the English Church, 1640–1660*, 2 vols. (1900).

Alan Simpson, *Puritanism in Old and New England* (Chicago, 1955; Cambridge, 1956; Phoenix paperback).

M. Walzer, *The Revolution of the Saints* (Cambridge, Mass., 1965; London, 1966).

A. S. P. Woodhouse (ed.), *Puritanism and Liberty* (1938): good Introduction, and illustrative documents.

VII

Scientists and Society

H. F. KEARNEY

The term 'The Scientific Revolution' is by now a familiar one. We have come to see that the intellectual changes which took place in Western Europe during the sixteenth and seventeenth centuries amounted to a revolution in man's approach to the universe. The beginnings may be seen in the work of Copernicus in the field of astronomy. Copernicus' book on the heavens was published in 1543 but it took some time before his theory was accepted as a satisfactory alternative to the established view that the earth was the centre of the universe. Even Milton did not take the Copernican revolution into account in *Paradise Lost*. George Herbert, in his poem *Vanity*, was still moved by the old astronomy.

> The fleet Astronomer can bore
> And thread the spheres with his quick-piercing mind:
> He views the stations, walks from door to door,
>   Surveys, as if he had designed
> To make a purchase there: he sees their dances,
>   And knoweth long before,
> Both their full-eye'd aspects, and secret glances.[1]

It was not easy for the new Copernican view to replace the old traditional view, which was embedded in the Bible and in philosophy. Since the thirteenth century, scholars had created a complex structure of doctrine out of the Old and the New Testaments, the early Fathers, and ideas derived from Aristotle and ancient Greek philosophy. This structure still held a dominant position, even as late as 1650. It was criticized on all sides but it had the advantage over its rivals of being in possession of the field. Aristotle's ideas

[1] Quoted in R. Lamson and H. Smith, *Renaissance England* (1956), p. 896.

were based on simple notions of growth and decay, matter and form, which since the thirteenth century had formed an essential part of the European mind. The passage of time had scarcely weakened its intellectual sway. The reformation left Aristotle's scientific influence undisturbed. The Catholic revival of the second half of the sixteenth century gave Aristotelianism a new lease of life. At the Council of Trent the Jesuits used the vocabulary of Aristotle to define the truths of the Roman Catholic Church and they extended the influence of Aristotle in their own universities and colleges.

It was only as late as the sixteen-forties that Aristotelianism as a philosophy was forced on to the defensive. New ideas came flooding in, of which the most influential were those of Galileo and René Descartes. In 1633 Galileo was condemned in Rome for teaching Copernican theories, but this gave only temporary relief for the established doctrines. In 1637 Descartes published his *Discourse on Method* in which he challenged the doctrines of Aristotle and emphasized the importance of mathematics. By the time Descartes' later works were published in the sixteen-forties, European intellectuals were faced with a choice between the system of Aristotle which was based on logic and that of Descartes which relied on mathematics. For a time the issue was in doubt, but by 1700 the decision had been made. Aristotle was everywhere in retreat and mathematics was in the ascendant, although by then the influence of Descartes in turn was giving way to that of Isaac Newton. The scientific revolution was complete. Alexander Pope, writing in the 1720s, celebrated the final victory of the new ideas in two famous lines.

> Nature and Nature's Laws lay hid in night
> God said 'Let Newton be' and all was light.[2]

So far, so good. But what I have said is of course over-simplified, though it must be put in this way if we are to get the scientific revolution in perspective. If we look upon the fifteen hundred years from Aristotle to Copernicus as an intellectual whole, the scientific revolution marks the first unmistakeable breach. But when we come down to detail, the perspective changes, and our wonderfully clear

[2] Alexander Pope, *Epitaphs*.

picture of the scientific revolution dissolves into many fragments, all clamouring for our attention. Even the very notion of 'revolution' loses its sharpness of outline. The changes which Copernicus began in 1543 took over a century and a half to come to fruition and then they only affected the intellectual attitudes of a small fraction of the population. These changes were confined to certain aspects of astronomy and mechanics. We tend to exaggerate the effect of the scientific revolution, often on the basis of poetic evidence such as the lines John Donne wrote in 1611.

> And new Philosophy calls all in doubt,
> The Element of fire is quite put out;
> The Sun is lost, and th' earth, and no man's wit
> Can well direct him where to looke for it.[3]

But, when it came to the point, those people who accepted Christian doctrines were no more in doubt than they had been before. For Christians, human life had always seemed uncertain and insecure in comparison with the next life. In 1626, some fifteen years later, Donne, now a canon of St. Pauls, pointed out that he had no need of the 'new philosophy' to illustrate the transience of earthly values.

> I need not call in new Philosophy, that denies a settledness, an acquiescence in the very body of the Earth, but makes the Earth to move in that place, where we thought the Sun had moved; I need not that help, that the Earth it self is in Motion, to prove this, That nothing upon Earth is permanent; The Assertion will stand of it self, till some man assign me some instance, something that a man may rely upon, and find permanent.[4]

The truth is that we must think in terms of a slower rate of change and a more complicated picture than the poets and scientists themselves would have us believe.

The slow pace of change was in part related to social conservatism It is hard for us to believe that most men in 1600 accepted the political and social inequality of mankind as one of the facts of nature. When

[3] John Donne, 'The First Anniversary', quoted in *Renaissance England*, p. 816.
[4] John Donne, Sermon of 1626, quoted in *Renaissance England*, p. 831.

they looked at the natural world, they saw hierarchy everywhere from God downwards. During the sixteenth century political writers like Sir Thomas Elyot, an influential humanist, upheld beliefs in a ruling élite by pointing to the arrangements made in nature.

> Behold also the order that God hath put generally in all his creatures beginning at the most inferior or base, and ascending upward . . . so that every kind of tree, herbs, birds, beasts, and fishes . . . [are disposed] so that in everything is order and without order may be nothing stable or permanent.[5]

It followed from this that if order was taken away, chaos would follow. The Book of Homilies made the same points to a wider public from 1547 onwards.What all this amounted to was that scientific thought was inextricably mingled with political thought. Science was not something remote and academic. It was part of the politics and political attitudes of everyday life. If we look for a present day example we might turn to some of the southern areas of the United States of America. In Tennessee, Darwin's theory of evolution was a live issue in the nineteen-twenties (and still is for many) because it contradicted the teaching of Genesis on which the doctrine of racial inequality was believed to rest.

In early seventeenth-century England, to tamper with the accepted world picture was not a neutral activity. It implied critical attitudes in the world of politics. In the fifteen-nineties the Anglican apologist, Richard Hooker, attempted to answer the Puritans by arguing that their disobedience to law was unnatural, since it went against the ingrained obedience of the world, which the stars, and sun itself demonstrated.

> If celestial spheres should forget their wonted motions . . . if the prince of the lights of heaven which now as a giant doth run his unwearied course, should, as it were, through a languishing faintness begin to stand and rest himself. . . . what would become of man himself . . .? See we not plainly, that obedience of creatures unto the Law of nature is the stay of the whole world?[6]

[5] Thomas Elyot, *The Governor* (Everyman Library), p. 3.
[6] R. Hooker, *Laws of Ecclesiastical Polity* (1830), i. 76.

But suppose the world was not like this? Suppose the sun did not move? Suppose there were no spheres? All the ideas about the world which man accepted as absolutely true would be called into question. And with them, the acceptance of hierarchy as a fact of nature. It was small wonder that there was a general reluctance to reconsider the natural scheme of things which the Greek scientists handed down. Conservatism was the common sense attitude, as it was in the days of Darwin later on. It so happened that common sense was wrong.

After all this, some readers may well doubt whether the scientific revolution took place at all in the seventeenth century. Of course they would be mistaken. All I have been suggesting is that the pace of change was slow and that the discoveries as they were made affected a comparatively small number of people. The discoveries were not labelled 'scientific—to be enjoyed at leisure'; the actual scientific fact itself was always bound up with the views about the world which the majority of people would find unacceptable. Political conservatism, religious orthodoxy, the prejudices of common sense—all these played their part in confining the revolutionary side of science to a few minds.

There is also the point that the discoveries for which Copernicus, Kepler and Galileo were responsible, were not of themselves self-evident truths. They were highly technical innovations which were difficult for most people to grasp. Not that the scientists themselves were as clear-headed as we tend to think! Kepler's view of the universe may be described not unfairly as a mystical one. In fact, it seems to have been precisely this mysticism which led him on to fresh discoveries. We should not be surprised that his critics took his notions less seriously than he did himself and dismissed them all as a farrago of eccentricity. A letter from the Puritan Lord Conway written in 1651, illustrates the kind of criticisms that were levelled at scientists like Harvey and Descartes.

Daughter,

 . . . I hear that you have great good opinion of Doctor Harvey. I think you do well to love and respect a person of his merit for I think he hath deserved extremely well of all learned men, for what he hath found out, or offered to the world to enquire farther into: he is a most excellent Anatomist, and I conceive that to be his Masterpiece, which knowledge is many times of very great use in consultations, but in the practical parte of Physicke I conceive him to be too much, many times, governed by Phantasy, the excellency and strength whereof did produce his two works to the world, and he is not the only man that hath produced works in that nature, De Cartes and Campanella, but the first especially, have written as their phantasy did persuade, and done as a man must do that goes on hunting in a thick enclosed country, leave his horse behind him and scramble over hedge and ditch and tear his clothes, so do they leave the ancient rules, and set up new opinions for the maintenance of which, they are forced to great inconveniences, in their reason, when they are brought to the Practice.[7]

Everywhere in early seventeenth-century science, we find themes of magic and the occult. They were not distinct from science; they were part of it. And in a sense it was the Aristotelians who were the sober rationalists. Imagination was the prerogative of the visionaries who looked beyond the end of their noses and saw a world which contradicted the evidence of their senses.

There is another qualification which we must make to accepted views. It seems natural for us to assume that England led Europe in the field of science at this time. This is a point of view which many historians unconsciously adopt, that is, providing they are Englishmen. But closer scrutiny of the scientific revolution leads us to consider the rôle played by the other nations of Europe. As well as the Englishman Isaac Newton there was the German scientist Kepler, the Italian astronomer Galileo and the French mathematician Descartes. If we look more closely at England we will find a whole host of other English scientists come into focus, but this should not lead us to assume that the same phenomena would not occur for France, Italy, Holland or Germany. Scientific activity was European in its scope, not merely English.

English scientists came late into the field but when they did appear

[7] Letter of Lord Conway to his daughter, 1651. *The Conway Letters*, ed. M. Nicolson (1930), p. 30.

their brilliance was undeniable. The astronomers Horrocks and Hailey and the chemist Boyle are merely the best known of two gifted generations. On the whole, the richest period was in the second half of the seventeenth century, though in the first half we find William Harvey, who discovered the circulation of the blood, and William Gilbert, who worked out the scientific implications of magnetism. Two dates stand out: the foundation of the Royal Society in 1662 and the publication of Newton's *Principles of Natural Philosophy* in 1687, which brought the work of Galileo and Kepler into a common framework.

These decades were the Golden Age of English science. If we ask why these years were particularly fruitful several explanations are possible. If we wish, we may seek the explanation in providence and see Newton and his contemporaries as an uncovenanted blessing, a crop of genius which falls to every nation some time or another. But there is something unsatisfactory in relying solely on this kind of approach. We are surely entitled to ask why at this time so many gifted individuals decided to devote themselves to scientific activity. The pursuit of so arduous and often unrewarding an activity as the study of nature requires a good deal of explanation. Some scientists found it difficult to persevere. Christopher Wren, for example, made his mark in science while still a young man, but in his maturity he turned away from science to architecture. In doing this he was following an accepted tradition: the pursuit of art and the cultivation of the beautiful enjoyed a recognized prestige in Europe. By contrast science could appear as odd, eccentric, even irreligious. Thus the decision to engage in science rather than sticking to safe professional work requires some explanation in social terms. How did it come about that seventeenth-century England, in so many ways a static and conservative society, produced so many scientists during this period?

For some historians, the answer is a simple one. They see science as one of a number of so-called progressive movements in seventeenth-century England, an England already divided between progressives and conservatives. Puritanism, trade, and science are seen as inter-connected and inter-related. On this showing, the Civil War itself was a struggle between the traditional Aristotelians and the radical Copernicans. The Royalists stood for the old world, the Puritans for the new.

This view rests upon several assumptions. In the first place it assumes that we can distinguish clearly between progressives and reactionaries, that English scientists like Francis Bacon for example were Puritans, and that Puritanism itself was necessarily forward looking (whatever that means). There is no space to deal with this argument extensively here, but one or two points are worth comment. First of all the notion that Francis Bacon was a Puritan. Bacon was the first great popularizer of scientific ideas in this country. To be sure, his mother was a Puritan, but Bacon himself, like many other sons of zealots, seems to have reacted against this background. He showed little sympathy for the Puritans, if we judge by the advice he gave to Buckingham in 1616.

> Besides the Roman Catholics, there are a generation of sectaries, the Anabaptists, Brownists, Familists, Scripturists and many other of that kind. They have been several times very busy in this kingdom under the colourable pretensions of zeal for the reformation of religion. The King your master knows their dispositions very well; a small thing will put him in mind of them; his Majesty had experience of them in Scotland, I hope he will beware of them in England; a little countenance or connivance sets them on fire.
>
> Order and decent ceremonies in the Church are not only comely but commendable; but then there must be great care taken not to introduce innovations. They will quickly prove scandalous. Men are naturally over-prone to superstition; the true Protestant religion is settled in the golden mean; the enemies unto her are the extremes on either hand.[8]

This quotation suggests that Bacon's views on religion were similar to those of James I: protestant certainly but not Puritan.

Similar difficulties arise if we describe seventeenth-century scientists as inevitably progressive. Bacon's contemporary William Harvey, for example, was Aristotelian to the core, and as conservative in politics as in philosophy. And William Oughtred, one of the most

[8] Bacon, *Works*, ed. J. Spedding (1857–74), vi. 32.

influential mathematicians of the early seventeenth century, was fascinated by magic and the occult and in this he was no exception. This was hardly the mark of a progressive. John Aubrey describes him in a contemporary sketch.

> [William Oughtred] was an Astrologer, and very lucky in giving his Judgements on Nativities; he confessed that he was not satisfied how it came about that one might foretell by the Stars, but so it was that it fell out true as he did often by his experience find; he did believe that some genius or spirit did help. . . . He was a great lover of Chemistry, which he studied before his son Ben can remember, and continued it; and told John Evelyn, of Detford, esq., not above a year before he died, that if he were but five years (or three years) younger, he doubted not to find out the Philosopher's stone. It was made of the harshest clear water that he could get, which he let stand to purify, and evaporated by simmering.[9]

On the basis of the evidence, it looks as if we cannot explain the scientific revolution in terms of simple relationship between Puritanism, science and an emerging middle class. We may look for some sort of pattern but of a different and more subtle kind. We must begin by changing our notion of the scientific revolution.

As I suggested at the beginning, the scientific revolution was not a simple event but a complicated series of different events. Even the idea of science in our sense didn't exist. The term science included much that we would regard as unscientific. This was Francis Bacon's description of three sciences:

> Astrology, Natural Magic and Alchemy of which sciences . . . the ends are noble. For astrology pretendeth to discover that correspondence . . . which is between the superior globe and the inferior: natural magic pretendeth to call and reduce natural philosophy from variety of speculations to the magnitude of works: and alchemy pretendeth to make a separation of all the unlike parts of bodies which in mixtures of nature are incorporate.[10]

[9] Aubrey, John, *Brief Lives,* ed. O. Dick (1949), pp. 223–4.
[10] Bacon, *Works,* iii. 289.

Much of what we call science, Bacon called 'history', using the word in its original sense of enquiry. Thus for him Natural History meant enquiry into nature. He also distinguished between liberal arts and mechanical arts, between liberal sciences and mechanical sciences, as well as between science and philosophy. But of almost equal importance were the social distinctions which men, following the Greeks, had created among their intellectual activities. Bacon was undoubtedly aware of this.

> I have set down at length all experiments of the mechanical arts, of the operative parts of the liberal arts, of the many crafts which have not yet grown into arts properly so called. . . . Nay (to say the plain truth) I do in fact (low and vulgar as men may think it) count more upon this part both for helps and safeguards than upon the other seeing that the nature of things betrays itself more readily under the vexations of art than in its natural freedom.[11]

The key words here are 'low and vulgar as men may think it'. The division in English society, between gentlemen and common people, rested in large measure upon those who didn't work with their hands and those who did. This division was perpetuated in education, in medicine and hence in science itself.

The consequences which followed from these social divisions were important. Some aspects of nature were treated as part of a sophisticated intellectual tradition, while other aspects were considered trivial. Astronomy for example, as one of the liberal arts, was exposed early to contact with the universities and hence with mathematics. On the other hand chemistry fell within the province of apothecaries and alchemists and developed on less sophisticated lines. The intellectual value put on any particular scientific activity determined its social status and the number of educated gentlemen who would be drawn to it.

Thus the social status of different intellectual disciplines had an important effect on their rate of development and on their manner of development. At the beginning of the seventeenth century, alchemy for example, was placed low on the social scale, as we see in Ben

[11] *ibid.*, p. iv. 29.

Jonson's *Alchemist* which poked fun at the alchemists for their lack of breeding.

But in the second half of the seventeenth century the rigidities of social status among the different approaches to nature tended to dissolve, though they did not entirely disappear. The foundation of the Royal Society in 1662 brought together alchemy and physics on to the same social level. This fulfilled Bacon's hope that experiments involving manual dexterity, like alchemy, should not be excluded from science. The Royal Society became the patron of the laboratory as well as the library. The effect of its foundation was to bring science into the social swim. Of course aristocratic patrons of science are to be found as early as the sixteenth century, but at that time they were exceptional. For the mass of the gentry were brought up in the Renaissance tradition of education, which accentuated the differences between the liberal arts and the mechanical arts. To the ears of the gentry the word 'mechanical' had a socially derogatory ring about it. A great chemist like Robert Boyle, son of the first earl of Cork, braved the social sneers of his contemporaries and made his mark in chemistry. But had he not been the son of an aristocrat, he probably would not have been the Father of Modern Chemistry. The Royal Society eventually both broke down the barriers between theoretical and practical science, and brought the gentry and the new scientists together in close intellectual contact. At last science was made respectable. One result of this was that more money became available for the achievement of scientific research. Patronage of science undoubtedly existed in the first half of the seventeenth century, but so far it had tended to be on a small scale compared with the large sums devoted to philanthropic activities. From 1662 the patronage given under the auspices of the Royal Society meant that scientific experiments could now be regularly conducted.

But all this patronage would have counted for little had not a scientific movement already existed on a small scale within the University of Oxford. Oxford in the mid-seventeenth century provided a refuge for intellectuals seeking shelter from the turbulent world of politics.

It was therefore, some space after the end of the Civil Wars at *Oxford* in *Dr. Wilkins* his Lodgings, in Wadham College, which was then the place of Resort for Vertuous, and Learned Men, that the first meetings were made, which laid the foundation of all this that follow'd. The *University* had, at that time, many Members of its own who had begun a *free way* of reasoning; and was also frequented by some *Gentlemen*, of Philosophical Minds, whom the misfortunes of the Kingdom, and the security and ease of a retirement amongst Gown-men, had drawn thither. Their first purpose was no more, they only had the satisfaction of breathing a freer air, and of conversing in quiet one with another, without being engag'd in the passions, and madness of that dismal Age. And from the Institution of that *Assembly*, it has been enough, if no other advantage had come, but this: That by this means there was a race of young Men provided, against the next Age, whose minds receiving from them, their first Impressions of *sober* and *generous knowledge*, were invincible arm'd against all the enchantments of Enthusiasm.[12]

In this passage Thomas Sprat suggests to us that scientists were not part of a broad and progressive social movement, but rather that they were alienated from society. This need not surprise us. It may well be that the scientific study of nature implies some measure of abstraction from the day-to-day world of man. It is rarely that we find a scientist who is also an active politician, and what is true of our own day is equally true of seventeenth century.

What of the second generalization, the idea that Puritanism, capitalism and science were interconnected? Can we offer an alternative interpretation?

I would certainly reject the idea that the Puritan Revolution directly fostered the growth of science. Thomas Sprat writing to Christopher Wren in 1658 described what had become of Gresham College in this period of social unrest.

This day I went to visit Gresham College but found the Place in such a nasty condition, so defil'd and the smells so infernal that if you should now come to make use of your Tube, it would be like Dives looking out of Hell into Heaven. Dr. Goddard, of all your Colleagues keeps possession which he could never be able

12 Thomas Sprat, *History of the Royal Society* (1667), p. 53.

to do, had he not before prepar'd his Nose for camp perfumes, by his voyage into Scotland, and had he not such excellent Restoratives in his cellar. The soldiers by their violence which they put on the Muses Seats have made themselves odious to all the ingenious world; and if we pass by their having undone the Nation, this crime we shall never be able to forgive them.[13]

On the other hand the effect of the Revolution may have been to induce men to see science as a refuge from Puritan politics. In other words, its effect was to bring together, in isolation from politics, intellectuals whose energies would have otherwise been dissipated. It may sound far-fetched but we may see in the pursuit of astronomy men seeking the same refuge from the hard realities of Cromwellian England, as poets sought in the writings of pastoral lyrics.

As another factor influencing the scientific revolution we may also consider the contact which English scientists enjoyed with European currents of thought. During the middle decades of the seventeenth century European science provided a valuable stimulus—the mathematical speculations of Descartes and the new experimental techniques of Pascal, for example. These and other sources helped to counteract the unmathematical and amateurish heritage of Francis Bacon. Bacon's genius is undoubted, but he knew no mathematics and his experiments were unsophisticated by the standards of half a century after his death. As every schoolboy knows, he died as the result of an experiment. Bacon himself told the story in his last letters but John Aubrey gives us all the details.

> Mr. Hobbes told me that the cause of his Lordship's death was trying an experiment viz as he was taking the air in a coach with Dr. Witherbourne . . . towards Highgate, snow lay on the ground and it came into my Lord's thoughts why flesh might not be preserved in snow, as in salt. They were resolved they would try the experiment presently. They alighted out of the coach and went into a poor woman's house at the bottom of Highgate Hill and bought a Hen and made the woman exenterate it, and then stuffed the body with Snow, and my Lord did help

[13] Letter from Thomas Sprat, 1658, quoted in C. Wren, *Parentalia* (1750), p. 254.

to do it himselfe. The snow so chilled him that he immediately fell so extremely ill that he could not return to his Lodging . . . but went to the Earl of Arundel's house at Highgate where they put him in a good bed warmed with a pan but it was a damp bed . . . which gave him such a cold that in 2 or 3 days as I remember Mr. Hobbes told me he died of suffocation.[14]

But of course to call this an experiment is an abuse of words. Bacon was a scientific enthusiast of an interesting kind, not a skilled experimenter. It was from the continent that England derived the experimental skills which led to the achievements of the second half of the seventeenth century.

There is room for one final word about the scientific revolution. It may well be that we are tempted to over-estimate its importance. Perhaps in the long run the new critical methods of seventeenth-century historians like Casaubon in France were more revolutionary than the mathematics of Newton. Mathematics after all was part of the Greek inheritance, whereas historical criticism was a new force unknown to the Greeks. In the face of the humanists' historical criticisms, the Bible changed its character, the accepted body of Roman law dissolved into fragments and ultimately even the apparently timeless universe of Newton was called into question.

Books for further reading

H. Butterfield, *Origins of Modern Science* (1950).

G. C. Gillispie, *The Edge of Objectivity* (1960).

J. E. C. Hill, *Intellectual Origins of the English Revolution* (1965).

R. F. Jones, *Ancients and Moderns* (1936).

H. F. Kearney (ed.), *Origins of the Scientific Revolution* (1964).

R. K. Merton, *Science, Technology and Society in Seventeenth Century England* (reprinted 1968 from *Osiris* iv, 1938).

M. Nicolson, *Science and Imagination* (1957).

B. Willey, *The Seventeenth Century Background* (1934).

[14] Aubrey, *Brief Lives*, p. 16.

VIII

Social Change and the Law

E. W. IVES

Lawyers have never been among the best loved members of any community. Yet in the two centuries which preceded the English Civil War, criticism of the legal profession was particularly acute. The long tradition of social comment (from More, Elyot and Starkey, through the great preachers of the mid-sixteenth century, like Latimer or Lever, to the moralists of Elizabeth's reign and the early seventeenth century) anathematized the lawyers, while in more plebeian vein, common proverb and ancient saw testified to their unpopularity. The more cunning the lawyer, the higher his fee, and inevitably the poor came off worst; delay after delay ensured that the wealth of the client passed into the pocket of his lawyer; judges, counsel, attorneys and court officials could be corrupted by influence, intimidated by social pressure or, quite simply, bribed—accusations such as these were commonplace. The lawyer's calling was essentially that of a parasite. As a proverb first recorded in 1627 put the matter 'if you go to law for a nut, the lawyers will crack it, give each of you half the shell and chop up the kernel themselves.' A satire of 1641, *News from Rome, Hell and the Inns of Court*, describes a feast provided by the devil for the pope. The dishes include:

> a large golden charger, containing a very great number of base-minded, covetous, unjust, extorting and oppressing lawyers, who value every word, by them uttered at a bar of justice, at a far higher price, than His Holiness does his bulls, issued forth for remission of sins; and these caterpillars his Majesty King Lucifer hath brought into such great esteem with all the inhabitants of England, as that no man of quality thinks his house to stand,

unless it be supported by one of those vermin pillars and brood of contention.[1]

This fierce criticism of the lawyers is not entirely explained by their sharp practices, nor by the dislike of laymen for something they do not understand. The sheer volume of complaint is, rather, a measure of the position which lawyers had come to occupy in English life. The most notorious aspect of this was their success in acquiring land and social advancement. Between James I's accession and the calling of the Long Parliament, fourteen men presided over the courts of King's Bench and Common Pleas at Westminster; of these chief justices, two were created earls and one a baron, the families of five more were later raised to the peerage, and another four established dynasties of landed gentry which endured into the nineteenth century. Tales lost nothing in the telling. The attorney-general, Edward Coke, was credited with having an income of £12,000 a year, while his first wife brought him a dowry of £30,000. For an intelligent man, a career as attractive as the law was difficult to find. The church had little to offer, not everyone was suited or had the necessary entrée to be a merchant, while the royal court, offering though it did the most glittering prizes, was hardly a haven of security. But England—unlike France—put no barrier between lawyers and gentry, and a career in law became the most important source of the wealth which enabled new men to break into landed society, or more frequently, a smaller squire to rise in the world and younger sons of gentlemen to overcome their lack of any patrimony. Gentlemen swarmed in ever increasing numbers to the Inns of Court where they rubbed shoulders with the established members of the profession and went as far in training as fancy or ambition took them.

But lawyers were important for a second reason. Laws mirror the structure of a community, and as the community develops, so the law will need to change. This can be readily seen in legislation. After the Reformation, there was a wave of enthusiasm for the endowment of secular charities and, consequently, in 1601, the trust laws were codified in a major act of parliament which was to remain on the

[1] *News from Hell, Rome and the Inns of Court* (1641), printed in *Harleian Miscellany* (1808–11), vii. 219.

statute book until 1888. But until relatively recent times, reform of the law by legislation was unusual. English law was predominantly case law, the aggregate of past judicial decisions, only slightly modified by statute. Hence, when new problems arose—and changes in economic life and society in the sixteenth and seventeenth centuries made these plentiful—they had to be dealt with by analogy with or development from past judgements. To argue from medieval precedent to seventeenth-century reality was not easy; often there was no real precedent, and lawyers had to burrow into the ancient records for something which could serve their purpose, which explains their preoccupation with the law and law-books of the middle ages and the far-fetched arguments which they used. But the consequence was that the courts, judges and counsel, not parliament, had the real task of changing the law, and the opportunity, by favouring this construction or impeding that, to shape society. For example, sixteenth-century landowners found capital difficult to raise, either to develop property or to establish in the world their daughters and younger sons. A landlord could borrow on short term against the security of his property, but existing law made this very hazardous; a mortgage was almost a sale mitigated only by a very limited opportunity to redeem the property. Gradually, however, the law was changed in response to the needs of society, and between 1615 and 1630 began to protect the title of the borrower who kept up interest payments, even though the capital was still outstanding. Thereafter, long loans could be raised securely, and men who before would have sold land to raise cash, were now able to preserve their estates intact and borrow upon mortgage. The resilience and continuity of landed fortunes during the next century and a half, was, in part, a consequence of this change in the law.

Since lawyers were one with the propertied classes, such changes, not surprisingly, often favoured business interests. This can be clearly seen in the important issue of monopolies. In the late sixteenth and early seventeenth centuries, a patent of monopoly might be given to safeguard a new invention, but far more usually it was a form of disguised sales tax. An individual was given the sole right to manufacture a product—gold and silver thread was a notorious example—or to trade in some commodity; he had no intention of going into business, but the patent gave him the right to compel those who were to pay him a royalty. The resulting inter-ference with trade was much resented, and as a government hard pressed for money made more and more frequent use of the patent to reward civil servants and courtiers and to buy off creditors, resentment became vocal. In the 1601 parliament, agitation against monopolies produced the biggest storm which Elizabeth ever had to face. But far more effective than parliamentary agitation was the increasing tendency of the courts in the last decade of the sixteenth century to treat monopolies as essentially repugnant to the common law: to harmonize, in fact, with the views of the gentry in the House of Commons. Ultimately, in the case of *Darcy versus Allein* of 1603, over the monopoly of the manufacture, import and sale of playing cards, the judges declared that a royal patent was void in law.

> The sole Trade of any Mechanical Artifice, or any other Mono-poly, is not only a Damage and Prejudice to those who exercise the same Trade, but also to all other Subjects, for the End of all these Monopolies is for the private Gain of the Patentees. . . . There are three inseparable Incidents to every Monopoly against the Commonwealth, *Sc* That the Price of the same Commodity will be raised, . . . The 2d Incident to a Monopoly is, That . . . the Commodity is not so good and merchantable as it was before; . . . 3 it tends to the Impoverishment of divers artificers and others, who before, by the Labour of their Hands in their Art or Trade, had maintained themselves and their Families, who will now of Necessity be constrained to live in Idleness and Beggary.[2]

This pronouncement by the Queen's judges on one of the hottest issues of the day, also illustrates how easily changes in the law could have political implications. As counsel for Allein said, 'this case is a delicate one, touching on the sovereign's prerogative and the sub-ject's liberty, and must be argued with extreme caution.'[3] Another

[2] Edward Coke, *11 Report* (1738), fo. 867; as in all references to Coke's writing it is important to remember that he 'embroidered' judicial decisions with arguments of his own.

[3] Quoted in W. S. Holdsworth, *History of English Law* (1922–64), iv. 349 n.1.

example of this occurred a few years later affecting responsibility for the behaviour of royal officials. Bureaucratic activity had been much extended in the sixteenth century, but the individual's only remedy against injustice still remained a petition to the sovereign, the method employed in the peripatetic household government of medieval kings, but hardly appropriate to the sixteenth century. But from 1606, King's Bench began to offer the procedure of *mandamus* which in effect made royal officers answerable at common law. The leading case, the complaint of James Bagge, a Plymouth burgess, against the mayor and corporation for wrongful expulsion from the town council, was heard by Edward Coke, now Lord Chief Justice, in 1615. Bagge's rights were vindicated—but so too were the claims of the King's Bench, and its right to discipline royal officers. One of Coke's critics pointed out the political consequences.

> He doth as much as insinuate that this court is all sufficient in itself to manage the state; for if the King's Bench may reform any matter of misgovernment . . . it seemeth that there is little or no use, either of the King's royal care and authority exercised in his person and by his proclamations, ordinances and immediate directions, nor of the Council Table, which under the King is the chief watchtower for all points of government, nor of the Star Chamber, which hath ever been esteemed the highest court for extinguishment of all riots and public disorders and enormities.[4]

Lawyers, then, were important in the years before the revolution because of the part they played in society, and because their construction of the law had immense social and political implications. But there is a third reason—the position which the law occupied in English life. Land was bought and sold through the court of Common Pleas. Estates were still largely managed through manorial courts. Family life was dominated by legal considerations of inheritance, marriage and death. In the resulting atmosphere, going to law became second nature; litigation—his own or someone else's—was a passionate interest of the English gentleman. When the Essex diarist,

[4] Observations on Coke's Reports, pp. 11–12, quoted in E. G. Henderson, *Foundations of English Administrative Law* (1963), p. 70, n.41.

Sir Humphrey Mildmay, came to London, he looked forward to three pleasures, good food and drink, the society of pretty women and entertaining mornings at the law courts, watching the cases there. In public affairs also the law was of immense significance, for no clear distinction was made between administration and justice. At the provincial level, the court of quarter sessions dealt not only with crime, but with all the local government of a county and did so under judicial forms, so that the J.P. needed to be more than half a lawyer himself. The same was true at Westminster. Parliament was a court; a government department like the exchequer was a court and many civil servants were lawyers. When the king swore at his coronation to maintain the laws, this was more than a promise to eschew tyranny, it was a declaration that he would administer the country wisely. Whether in public or in private life, the law was inescapable in early Stuart England.

Yet the supreme significance of the law in the English Revolution remains to be mentioned. The law was the guardian of property and of the existing order of society. 'The common law,' declared Coke, 'is the best and most common birth-right that the subject hath, for the safeguard and defence, not only of his goods, lands and revenues, but of his wife, children, his body, fame and life also.'[5] This alone explains much of the pathological hatred of Strafford and the disgraceful campaign which hounded him to death in 1641. As Lord-Deputy in Ireland he had used royal authority to overbear common-law titles to property. The fact that many of these titles had been corruptly established at the expense of the crown and the church gave Strafford some moral justification, but English colonists in Ireland were drawn from the English landowning class and the common law which Strafford spurned in Ireland was identical with the common law which protected English estates. Because he represented this threat to stability, the judicial murder of Strafford seemed to the House of Commons imperative. Historians may like to say that king and parliament fought for control of the executive, or even over sovereignty; to contemporaries, law was the heart of the dispute. The indictment of Charles I alleged that:

[5] Edward Coke, *On Littleton*, 142a [ed. F. Hargrave and C. Butler (1794), Bk. 2, Ch. 12, Sect. 213].

the said Charles Stuart, being admitted King of England, and therein trusted with a limited power to govern by and according to the laws of the land, and not otherwise; . . . yet, nevertheless, out of a wicked design to erect and uphold in himself an unlimited and tyrannical power to rule according to his will, and to overthrow the rights and liberties of the people, . . .; he, the said Charles Stuart, for accomplishment of such his designs . . . hath traitorously and maliciously levied war against the present Parliament and the people therein represented.[6]

Charles prepared a reply to this, taking the same ground.

I speak not for my own right alone, as I am your King, but also for the true liberty of all my subjects, which consists not in the power of government, but in living under such laws, such a government, as may give themselves the best assurance of their lives, and property of their goods. . . . What hope of settlement is there so long as power reigns without rule or law, changing the whole frame of that government under which this kingdom hath flourished for many hundred years? . . . by this time it will be too sensibly evident that the arms I took up were only to defend the fundamental laws of this kingdom against those who have supposed my power hath totally changed the ancient government.[7]

With the law so important, it is small wonder that lawyers abounded; not simply barristers, but attorneys, solicitors and many smaller fry, they flourished in business and private affairs as well as in the law courts, and particularly in administration and politics. Here the judges were in the limelight, for the Stuarts submitted questions both of policy and of royal prerogative to judicial scrutiny. The prosecution of John Hampden for refusing to pay ship money for Charles I's navy is only the most famous in a whole series of great test cases. The crown usually won. Opponents cried 'corruption', 'intimidation', but with less justification than is often thought.

[6] *Constitutional Documents of the Puritan Revolution, 1625–60,* ed. S. R. Gardiner (3rd edn., 1906), pp. 371–2.
[7] *ibid.,* pp. 375–6.

Of course the judges were not un-interested in royal approval. Partly this was a matter of fear (although only two judges were actually sacked for political reasons), but more often it was a question of profit—the king was the employer with the most to offer. When in 1634, Sir John Finch helped to extend the boundaries of the forest of Dean in the king's favour, a device which led to the systematic intrusion of forest law upon most of Essex and half of Northamptonshire, to say nothing of elsewhere, Finch was attempting to demonstrate how suitable he was for the vacant post of attorney-general. But it was not merely a question of self-interest. English law was traditionally favourable to the crown, and judges had never been independent; they were royal servants, 'lions under', that is, supporting 'the throne'. Moreover, construction of medieval precedent in favour of the crown was perfectly defensible. When in 1606, the merchant, John Bates, challenged the king's right to impose new customs dues, the legal arguments convinced even politically hostile lawyers. Add to this the fact that when precedents were confused, reason was often on the side of the king: the physical violence which Sir John Eliot and his cronies offered to the Speaker of the Commons in 1629 surely merited punishment. English judges in the early seventeenth century cannot be dismissed as either browbeaten or sycophantic; most were professionally able men, forced by circumstances to grapple with problems novel to their experience, and to do so under pressure from both sides.

If we must acquit the judicial bench as a whole of time-serving when it supported the crown, we must also avoid being too ready to credit with idealism the lawyers who defended the liberty of the subject; self-interest was active here also. Successful opposition to the crown was a way to attract attention. Thomas Egerton pleaded so powerfully against Elizabeth that, swearing he should never do so again, she made him her solicitor-general; ultimately he became James I's greatest chancellor. Several of the opposition lawyers of the sixteen-twenties became Charles' servants in the sixteen-thirties. Nor must the pressure of the rat-race and the influence of individual likes and dislikes be forgotten. Francis Bacon's determination to succeed led him to produce legal quibbles to help James I to circumvent the judges, while antipathy to Edward Coke coloured much of his thinking; equally, Coke struck constitutional poses at least in part out of hatred for Bacon and out of personal vanity. To such personal factors some historians have added professional rivalry. The Tudors had promoted the court of Chancery and prerogative courts like Star Chamber and Councils of the Marches and of the North, to supply deficiencies in the legal system; these enforced common law, and common lawyers provided the advocates and many of the judges and court officials, but their procedure was speedier than that of the ancient King's Bench or Common Pleas, and they were far more able to deal with new problems. But by the end of Elizabeth's reign, the older common law courts were reforming themselves, and then prerogative courts began to appear as business rivals attracting fees which could have benefited the judges of the common law. Dr. W. J. Jones, however, has recently shown that antipathy between 'common law' and 'prerogative' courts can easily be exaggerated, and that co-operation was the normal state of affairs. The famous battles of the common law against equity were quite exceptional. Yet the very fact that they were also famous fits them into our story. More important than the degree to which common law judges were at odds with the prerogative was the fact that they could appear to be at odds at all. The self-interest of barristers also set common-law and prerogative at odds. Those who represented clients who challenged royal actions might argue that the prerogative was delimited by the common law or else, seeking notoriety or driven by genuine political feeling, counsel might use the opportunity to comment adversely on royal policies. Furthermore, since it was the prerogative courts which punished crimes against the state, and enforced especially the personal rule of Charles I between 1629 and 1640, support for the common law courts could easily become an opposition rallying cry.

But the greatest single factor where the self-interest of all the common lawyers combined to embroil the profession in politics, was their antagonism to the church courts. Apart from their notorious abuses, church courts were objectionable to barristers who could not plead before them, and to common law judges whose monopoly of property litigation was infringed by the church's jurisdiction over wills and tithes. To the whole profession, canon law appeared an alien system, bristling with objectionable procedures such as enforced self-accusation, and lacking the safeguards of jury trial. Opposition to the crown inevitably followed, for since the Reformation the church courts had come under royal control and enforced the king's social and moral discipline for the state; to criticize ecclesiastical tribunals was now to reflect upon the crown, while to invoke the common law's long established right to determine the limits of clerical jurisdiction smacked of treason. Religious dissidents and others prosecuted in the church courts naturally appealed to the common law courts, and professional jealousy, to say nothing of the strong Puritan beliefs of some lawyers, ensured that there were always counsel to aid them. Puritans embroiled the common law in religious controversy, and the common law was quite prepared to take advantage of the opportunity to strike at a rival system.

But the self-interest of a conservative and narrow-minded professional clique is not the only characteristic of the lawyers who opposed the early Stuarts. If some lawyers could honestly read the ancient laws in favour of the crown, it was equally possible for others to construe them for the individual. The crown might argue, for example, that the imprisonment of the five knights in 1627 on a warrant issued by 'his majesty's special command' complied with the provision of Magna Carta that no freeman should be imprisoned 'except by the laws of the land', but there was substance in John Selden's plea that compliance with the charter must demand more than the issue of a duly authorized warrant. And this was more than a difference of legal opinion. Men of property could only rest secure when, as Oliver St. John, Hampden's counsel, said, 'justice runs in certain and known channels', but royal manipulation of the law was progressively replacing these known channels by, in effect, arbitrary discretion. However arguable amongst lawyers, an interpretation of the common law which allowed the king to extend customs duties, to increase the area under forest law and to apply the levy of ship money to inland counties never taxed before—and all this without the sanction of parliament—was to the gentry manifestly wrong and perilous.

The relationship between common lawyers, society and the English Revolution is supremely illustrated in the career of Edward

Coke. We have seen how his wealth exemplifies the social importance of the lawyers. He had a major hand in modernizing the
common law—it was Coke who appeared against the playing card
monopoly, it was Coke who gave judgement for James Bagge. Coke
also embodied in full measure the less attractive characteristics of the
profession—his defence of the common law was never wholly dis-
interested, and he often saw only what he wanted to see. A colleague
told him that 'he was not such a master of the laws as he did take on
him, to deliver what he list for law and to despise all others.'[8]
Nevertheless, Coke's unique authority, enshrined in his monumental
writings, shaped the law for two centuries. Coke emphasized, first
and last, the importance of the common law to society—individual
obligations and rights, royal prerogatives and duties, all should 'be
measured by the golden and straight mete-wand of the law, and not
the incertain and crooked cord of discretion'. It was not only business rivalry and vanity, but convictions like this which led Coke to
sabotage systematically the power of the church courts, criticize
Chancery, hamper the prerogative and make the novel claim that
judges should be independent of the crown. The issues appear plainly
in Coke's version of an interview he had with James I.

> The King said that he thought the law was founded upon reason,
> and that he and others had reason as well as the judges. To which
> it was answered by me, that true it was that God had endowed
> His Majesty with excellent science and great endowments of
> nature, but causes are not to be decided by natural reason, but by
> the artificial reason and judgement of law. With which the King
> was greatly offended, and said that then he should be under the
> law, which was treason to affirm, as he said; to which I said that
> Bracton saith, *quod Rex non debet esse sub homine sed sub Deo et
> lege.*[9]

'The king is not subordinate to any man, but to God, and to the
law'—small wonder that, in 1616, Coke was dismissed. But he was
not silenced. From 1621 he spoke again, in parliament, for the
opposition. Strafford might vow to see Charles I's power 'set out of

[8] Holdsworth, v. 433, n.8.
[9] *Constitutional Documents of James I*, ed. J. R. Tanner (1930), p. 187.

wardship and above the expositions of Sir Edward Coke and his law books', but in 1641, with Coke and Strafford both dead, it was Coke's view of the law which was vindicated.[10]

As a lawyer, Edward Coke stood head and shoulders above his generation, but he was not the only one who criticized the crown. James I said that 'ever since his coming to the Crown, the popular sort of Lawyers have been the men that most affrontedly in all Parliaments have trodden upon his Prerogative', and his son Charles agreed with him.[11] The lawyers provided the real leadership of the political opposition. Men of repute—John Selden as well as Edward Coke—they led the opposition in the parliaments of the sixteen-twenties, and theirs was the great triumph of the Petition of Right. During Charles I's personal rule, lawyers were prominent in the Providence Company, a colonizing or—more truthfully—a piratical corporation which served as a front for the Puritan opposition to the king. Lawyers made up one third of the Feoffees for Impropriations, the group which attempted, until suppressed in 1633, to extend patronage for Puritans within the church. Charles might rely on lawyers in royal service, blandishments might win others over, but when the Long Parliament met in November 1640, it was Oliver St. John who emerged amongst the leaders of the gentry against a government hostile to their interests. Within months, the prerogative courts were no more, royal interpretations of the law condemned and the king's judges disgraced. Common law, as understood by the gentry, was triumphant.

The story of the next twenty years forms an ironic comment on this victory. In 1642, Parliament had declared that, by the law, the nobility and gentry 'enjoy their estates, are protected from any act of violence and power, and differenced from the meaner sort of people, with whom, otherwise, they would be but fellow-servants.'[12] But as the nobility and gentry came to blows amongst themselves, 'the meaner sort of people' were able to raise their voices for the first time, and with the backing of the New Model Army. Far from being

[10] Quoted in C. V. Wedgwood, *Thomas Wentworth, Earl of Strafford* (1961), p. 402.
[11] British Museum, Hargrave Ms. 132, fo. 68ᵛ.
[12] *Journals of the House of Lords*, v. 258.

a guarantee of freedom for them, the common-law was their yoke of servitude. Levellers, Diggers and radicals of all sorts demanded the destruction of a legal system which perpetuated social privilege. Gerard Winstanley, leader of the semi-communistic Diggers, put the point with vigour.

> *England* is a Prison; and the varieties of subtelties in the Laws preserved by the Sword are bolts, bars and doors of the prison; the Lawyers are the Jailers; and poor men are the prisoners; for let a man fall into the hands of any, from the Bailiff to the Judge, and he is either undone, or weary of his life.
>
> Surely this power, the Laws, which is the great Idol that people dote upon, is the burden of the Creation, a Nursery of Idleness, luxury and cheating, the only enemy of Christ the King of righteousness; for though it pretend Justice, yet the Judges and Law-Officers buy and sell Justice for money, and wipes their mouths like *Solomon's* whore, and says it is my calling, and never are troubled at it.[13]

Far from deriving, as Coke and his colleagues had boasted, from the free institutions of the Anglo-Saxons, the common law had been imposed by the Norman Conquest; 'the tedious, unknown, and impossible-to-be-understood common law practices in Westminster Hall,' wrote one Leveller leader, 'came in by the will of a Tyrant, namely William the Conqueror.'[14] Magna Carta, another said, was 'but a beggarly thing, containing many marks of intolerable bondage'—a far cry from Coke's famous dictum that 'Magna Carta is such a fellow that he will have no "sovereign".'[15] The liberty which the common law preserved was liberty for the privileged few at the expense of the majority. William Cole, a radical sympathizer, asked:

> Is it not much for the advantage of the gentry, that seeing the laws are so corrupt and chargeable, they thereby can, and indeed have done, and in most parts do still keep the poor in such subjection, that [they] must run and go, and work, and obey them,

[13] Gerrard Winstanley, *Works,* ed. G. H. Sabine (New York, 1941), p. 361.
[14] Quoted in J. E. C. Hill, *Puritanism and Revolution* (1958), p. 76.
[15] *ibid.,* p. 76; J. Rushworth, *Historical Collections* (1721); i. 562.

as they shall please to command them, else they run the hazard of being undone.[16]

That there was much in the common law that needed reform, nobody could deny. Lawsuits were long-drawn-out and expensive affairs; the law was written partly in Latin and partly in bastard Norman-French and was unintelligible to the layman; procedure was excessively technical, while even lawyers could not always be certain what the law was. Often it was downright unjust. Money talked; a rich man could purchase a pardon for a really disgraceful crime, while a poor man would be hanged for petty theft. In civil litigation wealth could overcome the costly technicalities of the law, or even exploit these to advantage; the poor had to accept wrong which they could not afford to remedy. Indigent debtors might starve in the beggars' ward of a debtors' prison where the prosperous could shelter in comfort and evade paying their debts. Law reform, as men as diverse as Coke, Bacon, Raleigh and Cromwell all agreed, was a crying need.

But the radicals of the New Model Army and the Republic were not asking for reform, they demanded a new legal system to benefit a new class in society. Veneration for the existing law was, as William Cole pointed out, a delusion.

It is the usual cry and saying, both among the masters of oppression, the lawyers, and the ignorant people that know no better, that the laws of England are the safest and best laws in the world; and whosoever shall alter the said laws will unavoidably introduce a mischief instead of a benefit. But to those it is answered, that the major part of the laws, made in this nation, are founded upon principle of tyranny, fallacy and oppression for the profit and benefit of those that made them.[17]

Instead of the existing system, radicals offered programmes of their own. The Levellers sought the abolition of charters, privileges and titles, the reduction of the law to a small book of rules, written

[16] William Cole, *A Rod for the Lawyers* (1659), printed in *Harleian Miscellany*, iv. 321.
[17] *ibid.*, p. 319.

in English, and the establishment in every hundred of the kingdom of courts giving brief, simple justice, determined by twelve local men elected annually. If this had been achieved, the law would have ceased to support the existing hierarchy of rank and would, instead, have protected the interests of the substantial peasants and urban householders whom the Levellers represented.

But to the men of property, and these now numbered, as well as the older families, many who had come to wealth through the war, talk like this was anarchy and the ruin of society. Horrified by what they heard, the gentlemen resolutely set their faces against all change —better no reform than this—and their stand was heartily supported by the lawyers who had no intention of accepting redundancy. Although first the Rump and then Barebone's Parliament devoted considerable attention to legal problems with a commission which prepared a very worthwhile programme of reforms, nothing could in fact be done. The lawyers and gentlemen would not co-operate. There were, it is true, some improvements in the law in the years between the Civil War and the Restoration; English replaced the Latin and Norman-French: procedure was speeded up: imprisonment for debt was ameliorated, and legal fees pruned. Nevertheless, the shock of the plebeian challenge to law, and hence to property, impeded any really major changes in the law, long after the Levellers had been suppressed. Parliament might vote to abolish the court of Chancery, that 'mystery of wickedness and a standing cheat', but without expert guidance they did not know what to put in its place. When Cromwell tried to tackle Chancery reform, he too found that a layman's ideas—even those of a Lord Protector—would not work. The major abuses of the law remained.

But as the lawyers and gentlemen saw it, the common law had to be preserved, abuses and all, if property and the existing social order were to be preserved. Cromwell remarked 'we cannot mention the reformation of the law but they presently cry out, we design to destroy property; whereas the law as it is now constituted serves only to maintain the lawyers and to encourage the rich to oppress the poor'.[18] When Charles II returned in 1660, the courts reverted

[18] Quoted in J. E. C. Hill, *Intellectual Origins of the English Revolution* (1965), p. 264.

to their traditional Latin and Norman-French. Law reform was delayed for another two hundred years. This was the price the country paid to keep society safe for the men of property.

Books for further reading

J. W. Gough, *Fundamental Law in English History* (Oxford, 1955).

G. Hammersley, 'The revival of the forest laws under Charles I', in *History* xlv (1960).

A. Harding, *A Social History of English Law* (Penguin Books, 1966).

E. G. Henderson, *Foundations of English Administrative Law* (Harvard and O.U.P., 1963).

J. E. C. Hill, 'The Norman Yoke', in *Puritanism and Revolution* (1958).

J. E. C. Hill, *Society and Puritanism* (1964) [on church courts].

J. E. C. Hill, *Intellectual Origins of the English Revolution* (1965). [Sir Edward Coke].

E. W. Ives, 'The law and the lawyers', in *Shakespeare in his Own Age*, ed. Allardyce Nicoll (1964). [description of the legal system].

W. J. Jones, *The Elizabethan Court of Chancery,* (1967).

G. B. Nourse, 'Law reform under the Commonwealth and Protectorate', in *Law Quarterly Review*, lxxv (1959).

S. E. Thorne, *Sir Edward Coke, 1552–1952* (Selden Society, 1952).

D. O. Wagner, 'Coke and the rise of economic liberalism', in *Economic History Review*, 6 (1935). [monopolies].

The standard history of English law is W. S. Holdsworth, *History of English Law*, 14 vols., 1922–64. It is a work of immense importance, but has been modified by recent specialist work; a good introduction to this is provided by Harding.

IX

Class and Social Tension: the case of the merchant

BARRY SUPPLE

Most societies are too complex to be described in terms of all their individual variations. As a result, the categories which we use to discuss social affairs are always, more or less, abstractions. We are forced to think and talk about contemporary society, or social history, with the aid of general concepts—concepts like 'the bourgeoisie' or 'the working class'; 'teenagers' or 'university teachers'.

Of course, this habit of generalizing about economic and social groups is not peculiar to modern commentators on society. Here, for example, are the opening words (originally written in the sixteen-twenties) of Thomas Mun's *England's Treasure by Forraign Trade*:

> The love and service of our Country consisteth not so much in the knowledge of those duties which are to be performed by others, as in the skilful practice of that which is done by ourselves; and therefore (my Son) it is now fit that I say something of the Merchant, which I hope in due time shall be thy Vocation: Yet herein are my thoughts free from all Ambition, although I rank thee in a place of so high estimation; for the Merchant is worthily called The Steward of the Kingdom's Stock, by way of Commerce with other Nations; a work of no less *Reputation* than *Trust*, which ought to be performed with great skill and conscience, that so the private gain may ever accompany the public good.

In assuming the existence of a single class of merchants, and emphasizing their significance for England's economic development before the Civil War, Thomas Mun, was of course, doing no more than many modern historians have done. The changing economic and social position of merchant capitalists has figured very prominently in histories of pre-Civil War England. But how far did the merchants of early seventeenth-century England form a homogeneous class? To what extent did they have differing and even conflicting interests and allegiances? How wide were the divisions between merchants in general and other groups of society?

In fact, and in spite of Mun's rather special statement, the word 'merchant' covered a multitude of activities, and a multitude of interests. This was so, first because a 'merchant' was not simply a specialist in buying and selling commodities; second, because most of the economic activities of so-called 'merchants' could be undertaken at quite different scales of operation and with quite different results in terms of profit; and third, because the actual setting of these activities (in London or the provinces, in overseas or home trade) could vary to a significant extent and with significant consequences. Our picture of the seventeenth-century merchant must, therefore, be three-dimensional: taking account of variations in what he did, how successfully he did it and the setting in which he operated. Each of these might mask considerable differences in the merchant's view of the world around him—and of other merchants.

The first element in the resulting composite picture of the merchant group—the degree to which their actual economic functions varied—was a logical consequence of the level of economic development of Stuart England and of the commercial opportunities which it provided. In fact, the economy was too small and unstable for many men to be full-time specialists throughout their mercantile careers: the risks were too great. It was less risky, and on balance more profitable, to spread risks by diversifying investments. Traders therefore dabbled in insurance and shipowning, shipowners dabbled in finance and joint-stock investment, and wholesalers put their money into retailing and manufacturing. Further, businessmen who had accumulated capital by trading in commodities were constantly tempted into new fields of enterprise and investment, where the returns to substantial investment were better or safer. A particularly attractive field was moneylending. On the other hand, moneylending had two disadvantages from the viewpoint of other members of society. In the first place, it involved the taking of interest, or usury as it was then called—and the taking of interest, certainly excessive interest, was judged to be immoral and parasitical. Secondly, the tendency of merchants to leave commerce for finance was widely criticized as a means by which the field of productive enterprise was weakened: useful businessmen, it was felt, were becoming mere unproductive usurers. England was often contrasted with Holland in this respect—and the commercial greatness of the Dutch was frequently attributed to the fact that their mercantile dynasties were not tempted to leave the world of active and productive trade for pure speculation. This factor alarmed some observers at the time. In 1621, for example, Sir Thomas Culpepper complained about the temptations offered by the money market:

> We see that generally all merchants when they have gotten any great wealth, leave trading, and fall to usury, the gain thereof being so easy, certain and great. Whereas in other countries, where usury is at a low rate, and thereby lands dearer to purchase, they continue merchants from generation to generation, to enrich themselves and the State.[1]

Nor was it only the supposedly easy profits of private and public finance which attracted merchants. The temptations of landownership were also regarded as weakening the incentive to more productive effort. 'The City of London,' protested a member of parliament in 1621, 'is a place that seeks only to enrich themselves, and then away they go to the country in the second descent.'[2] Indeed, in a relatively stratified society in which landownership carried the highest status, there was an extraordinarily strong temptation to buy land. Given the further fact that security of investment was hard to achieve in other ways, so that a family fortune could be best preserved by sinking it in estates, that temptation was irresistible.

[1] *A Tract Against Usury* (1621), p. 23.
[2] *The Commons Debates of 1621*, ed. W. Notestein, F. H. Relf, and H. Simpson (New Haven, 1935), ii. 422.

Certainly most of the successful merchants we know about, succumbed to it. And, like *nouveaux riches* in every age, their social pretensions were the object of scorn and parody. It was, indeed, the social climbers among the merchants who provoked the most scathing criticisms from contemporary social moralists. Thus, in Thomas Middleton's play, *Michaelmas Term* (dating from the first decade of the century) the scheming woollen merchant, Quomodo, gulls an Essex gentleman out of his estates and proceeds to chuckle over his catch, his future and his new social position:

> O that sweet, neat, comely, proper, delicate, parcel of land! like a fine gentlewoman i' th' waist, not so great as pretty, pretty; the trees in summer whistling, the silver waters by the banks harmoniously gliding. I should have been a scholar; an excellent place for a student; fit for my son that lately commenced at Cambridge, whom now I have placed at Inns of Court. Thus we that seldom get lands honestly, must leave our heirs to inherit our knavery. . . . Now I begin to set one foot upon the land: methinks I am felling of trees already; we shall have some Essex logs yet to keep Christmas with, and that's a comfort.[3]

Yet moneylending and landownership were only two aspects of what merchants 'characteristically' did with their capital. For example, if we take the career of another Middleton—Sir Hugh Myddleton who died in 1631 at the age of 76—we find not only a cloth exporter and landowner, but a goldsmith, a cloth manufacturer, a pioneer of the New River water supply to London, a lessee of the Mines Royal, and a shareholder in the company which colonized Virginia. Lionel Cranfield (1575–1645) provides an equally spectacular example of economic diversification. He started life as an exporter of woollen cloth and an importer of continental goods. He then invaded the lucrative fields of leasing government concessions and lending money to an impecunious aristocracy. From being a part-time banker, Cranfield broadened out into speculating in customs administration and land purchase—ultimately becoming an official civil servant and Lord Treasurer of England. To make a

[3] Act II, scene iii (quoted in L. C. Knights, *Drama & Society in the Age of Jonson* (1937), p. 265.

lot of money in overseas commerce was often the beginning, rather than the end, of the most important chapter of a merchant's economic biography.

The examples of Hugh Middleton and Lionel Cranfield lead into the second aspect of this picture of the varieties of commercial capitalism in early Stuart England. For Middleton and Cranfield, together with their colleagues in the world of high finance and large-scale trading, were well-established and successful merchant–princes in London's commercial aristocracy. But the world in which they moved was small: it lay at the very tip of that pyramid of mercantile wealth, power and prestige which was itself merely part of the broader pattern of English society. Below such men were other merchants of smaller fortunes and more circumscribed fields of action: medium-scale exporters and importers, joint-stock investors to the tune of a few score pounds, wholesalers in a moderate way of business, routine financiers. And now and then we can catch a polemical echo of tensions which necessarily accompanied these differences in the scale of commercial operations.

In 1621, for example, in the middle of a period of depressed trade, the Staplers—the dealers in the raw material wool—tried to persuade parliament to pass a bill allowing them to participate in the export of manufactured cloth, until then a virtual monopoly in the hands of the Merchant Adventurers. For decades a relatively weak organization, the Staplers obviously hoped that they could revive their flagging fortunes by sharing some of the profits to be earned in the mainstream of England's trade. The regular traders were far from sympathetic! Here is part of the answer of the Merchant Adventurers, defending their privileges in that trade, with the claim that:

> the Staplers have of late years admitted into their fellowship for money a great number of wool broggers, clothiers and others unskilful in the trade of merchandizing. And yet further this bill enjoineth them to admit any of his Majesty's liegemen for ten pounds a man that shall desire to be free of their Company, so that their whole Company will consist of a multitude of unskilful traders, as fit for anything as for Merchandizing. This will in the first place discourage and drive out the skilful and substantial

merchants that usually bear a remainder of 20 or 30 thousand cloths upon their hands (and at this present between 30 or 40 thousand) and nevertheless continue their buying . . . but now will be caused to abandon the trade to the weak newcomers that are inferior to the burden.[4]

We have a situation, then, in which a worthy but plodding exporter of cheap cloth could share the name of 'merchant' with a dazzling 'operator' in the world of high finance and government contracting. And yet, as the complaint of the Merchant Adventurers indicated, the differences in the nature and scale of their operations could provoke fundamental differences in their outlook on matters of common concern. Indeed, in this case, as in others then and since, the apparent homogeneity of 'businessmen' as a group breaks down when closely observed. Common interests obviously existed, but businessmen operating at different levels of economic activity would take very different views of the market, of competition, and of economic privilege.

Similarly (and coming back to my third point), there were other basic differences between merchants which derived from the setting of their activities. Most notably, provincial traders or financiers could develop fundamentally different interests from those of London. This was especially so with regard to the great trade in cloth, in which the Merchant Adventurers occupied a privileged place, and which the provincial ports viewed with hopeless envy. As one pamphleteer put it:

> The Trade thus limited to a small number of a Company, residing for the most part at London, is a general prejudice to the whole Kingdom, which though it have made London rich, it hath made all the Ports and other parts of the Kingdom poor.[5]

And this view was widely shared. 'It is no good state,' said Sir Thomas Roe in 1640, 'for a body to have a fat head, thin guts, and lean members.' London merchants occupied a privileged position merely by virtue of their geographical location. They were at a major growth point of the economy: only rarely could they expect

[4] Notestein, Relf and Simpson, vii. 233.
[5] G. Malynes, *The Maintenance of Free Trade* (1622), p. 52.

amity rather than envy from their poorer 'fellow merchants' in the provinces.

Of course, these various factors tended to overlap. The opposition between provincial and London merchants, for example, frequently coincided with a clash between the relatively small-scale traders of the so-called 'outports' and the larger-scale merchants associated with the great trading companies of the metropolis. Again, those merchants who bought and sold goods on their own account (as they could do within the so-called 'regulated companies') could not always recognize the claims of joint-stock companies to centralized control of a privileged trade. This was a particularly sensitive issue at the time. The necessities of long-distance trade to places like Russia, America and the East Indies had introduced the joint-stock company, a new institution on the English commercial scene. But since joint-stock companies demanded, and generally secured, exclusive privileges to control particular trades, they generated a good deal of hostility. They came to be associated with the idea of 'monopoly' and it was to be many generations before the rest of the business community were resigned to their presence. As early as the parliament of 1604, for example, an attack was launched on the Muscovy Company (which controlled the trade with Russia and handled it as a single company):

> The Muscovy Company, consisting of eight-score or thereabouts, have Fifteen Directors, who manage the whole Trade; these limit to every Man the Proportion of Stock which he shall trade for, make One Purse and Stock of all, and consign it into the Hands of One Agent at Moscow, and so again, at their Return, to One Agent at London, who sell all, and give such Account as they please. This is a strong and a shameful Monopoly; a Monopoly in a Monopoly; both abroad and at home; a whole Company, by this Means, is become as One Man, who alone hath the Uttering of all the Commodities of so great a Country.[6]

This criticism of the Muscovy Company produced three reasons for believing the joint-stock arrangement to be harmful. The first

[6] *Tudor Economic Documents*, ed. R. H. Tawney and Eileen Power (1924), ii. 88–9.

claimed that a company encouraged Dutch competition; the second that it produced high prices. And the third argument touched the interest of smaller-scale traders, who owned shares in the company, who wanted a quick turnover, and who might suffer from their financial liability for failure by the company's agent:

> Thirdly, this is hurtful to all the young Merchants of their own Company, who cannot forbear their Stock so long as now they do, and desire to employ their own Industry in managing it, and having often times been all damnified by the Breaking of that general factor.

According to its proponents the Bill for free trade was supported by an overwhelming majority of merchants and manufacturers:

> The Committee from the House of Commons sat five whole afternoons upon these Bills; there was a great concourse of clothiers and merchants, of all parts of the realm, and especially of London; who were so divided, as that *all the clothiers, and, in effect, all the merchants of England, complained grievously of the engrossing and restraint of trade by the rich merchants of London*, as being to the undoing, or great hindrance, of all the rest; *and of London merchants, three parts joined in the same complaint against a fourth part; and of that fourth part, some standing stiffly for their own company, yet repined at other companies.*[7]

Of course, statements like these are not very surprising. It is a cliché of social analysis that men use their talents and capital in different ways, and that (as a result) their interests frequently conflict. What is interesting and important is the extent to which these conflicts could arise within a social grouping which is usually treated as a homogeneous class. On the other hand, we must still ask if all these divisions between so-called 'merchants' were indicative of really significant conflicts of economic and social interest? Or was their shared career as commercial capitalists—their common concern with mercantile and financial development—sufficient to unite them against the non-commercial elements of society? How much weight,

[7] *English Economic History: Select Documents*, ed. A. E. Bland, P. A. Brown and R. H. Tawney (1914), p. 443.

for example, should we put on theories that all merchants were on the side of parliament in the Civil War? Here is a contemporary analysis by a Royalist of the pattern of political allegiance:

> For the sea-coasts of the west, the great trading towns of Bristol, Lyme, Falmouth, Plymouth and Exeter (the king's navy being now under the command of the two houses), their interests as well as their inclinations made them parliamentarians . . . only the Cornishmen (as old bold Britons) were eminently loyal and royalist, although they had strong temptations to the contrary. The inland towns and cities in the west were most for the King.[8]

That there were some issues on which all—or nearly all—merchants could have a single opinion is perhaps too obvious a point to labour. But what seems more relevant is the extent to which their conflicts were real and deep and more or less continuous. The point here is that economic, social and political changes were creating rich openings for commercial enterprise. Here, for example, is Lionel Cranfield writing to a fellow merchant, while planning a 'corner' in the supply of imported dye-woods:

> One rule I desire may be observed between you and me, which is that neither of us seek to advance our estates by the other's loss, but that we may join together faithfully to raise our fortunes by such casualties as this stirring age may afford.[9]

But the 'casualties' to which Cranfield referred were paid for by other men—and other merchants. This would have been the case in the best conceivable circumstances: free competition produces constant conflict. But the conflicts of early Stuart England were aggravated by the fact that the world of commerce and finance was interpenetrated by privilege and by legal prohibition—by patents and monopolies, companies and licences, guaranteed markets and favoured relationships. The resulting restrictions on the operations of 'free enterprise' have led some historians to argue that a potentially

[8] Quoted in *The Good Old Cause,* ed. Christopher Hill and Edmund Dell (1949), pp. 247–8.
[9] A. F. Upton, *Sir Arthur Ingram* (1961), p. 17.

'capitalist' economy was being held in a 'feudal' strait-jacket, and that ultimately, through its frustration at royal policy, the merchant class united in resorting to violence to throw off the principal elements of 'feudal restriction'. But such an argument is really much too simple: one man's constraint is another man's privilege—one capitalist's loss is another's gain. Here, for example, is a petition from London and provincial merchants belonging to the Eastland (that is, the Baltic) Company dating from about 1630:

> To the Right Honourable the Lords and others of his Majesty's most Honourable Privy Council.
>
> That the company of late years have laboured under many difficulties and discouragements in their trade, first, heavy and insupportable losses at sea, secondly, the burdens and dangers of war seated in Prussia, the place of their trade, and lastly (which is not the least grievance) the excessive trade of clothiers and mariners outward, and other interlopers both subjects and strangers who daily import Eastland commodities, not only through the Sound of Denmark, but from Hamburg, Amsterdam and other places . . . .
>
> The petitioners therefore . . . do most humbly entreat the favour of this honourable Board, for the settling and confirming of their privileges at home, that clothiers, mariners and all other interlopers both inward and outward being restrained, they may cheerfully proceed in their trade as formerly. And as in duty bound they shall every pray etc.[10]

The Eastland merchants were successful in their petition, although not very successful in their subsequent trading. Indeed, none of the major assaults on commercial privileges achieved its object. Sooner or later those privileges were confirmed, as, for example, in 1634 when the Merchant Adventurers' cartel was sustained by a royal proclamation—at the price of opening its doors to any merchant who applied for membership. And a further interesting aspect of the Eastland Company's troubles was that although the threat from

[10] R. W. K. Hinton, *The Eastland Trade and the Common Weal* (1959), pp. 183–4.

outsiders was sufficient to unite Londoners and provincials, it did so only by widening the gap and tension between privileged and non-privileged economic interests.

Having said all this, however, it is obvious that there were deeper fissures in Stuart England than those I have been describing; and that there were overriding social tensions which diminished the significance of mercantile controversy. Yet even here merchants did not align themselves solidly on either side of the conflict over religion and politics which dominated the early seventeenth century. And even when they might have been reacting in ways determined by their economic interests, these interests (as we have seen) were too diversified to lead to any class unity in action. If most traders objected to higher customs duties not approved by any parliamentary sanction, there were sufficient wealthy merchants who had invested in the farming (i.e. sub-contracting) of customs collection to break any absolutely united front. If the City of London objected to pressures from Charles I to raise money on the eve of the war, there were enough merchants who had already lent substantial sums to him, or who were prepared to lend more, to prevent any unanimity of opinion. In 1640 and 1641, for example, the customs farmers helped raise vast amounts of money for Charles I.

This is not to deny that there were issues of taxing and finance on which at least the vast majority of merchants could agree; and to that extent, in general, merchant capitalists had opinions in common—as was illustrated in parliament's Grand Remonstrance of 1641:

> Tonnage and Poundage hath been received without colour, or pretence, of Law: many other heavy impositions continued against Law; and some so unreasonable, that the sum of the charge exceeds the value of the goods. The Book of Rates lately enhanced to a high proportion; and such merchants as would not submit to them illegal and unreasonable payments, were vexed and oppressed above measure . . . And, although all this was taken upon pretence of guarding the sea, yet a new and unheard-of tax of ship money was devised, upon the same pretence.[11]

[11] Thomas May, *The History of the Parliament of England . . . 1640* (1647; 1812), p. 242.

But this sort of problem occurred at a quite general level—and was, in any case, largely solved without hostilities. The far more complex, and less soluble, problems of England did not really co-incide with any easy division of occupational groupings into capital-ist and non-capitalist, merchant and non-merchant—or, for that matter, rising gentry and depressed gentry. Men did not kill each other because they belonged to different economic classes. Indeed, as we have already seen in relationship to the purchase of land by merchants, there was a sufficient degree of social mobility to obscure the divisions between different social groups.

And yet, having said all this, we should not too easily dismiss the historical relevance of the general concept of 'the merchant class', with its common interests and concerns. Indeed, even the question of privileges could be discussed in this way—as in the Introduction to *The Treasure of Traffic*, published in 1647 by a merchant, Lewes Roberts:

> I have lately discerned that our industrious Neighbours were ready at a dear rate to purchase that treasure by Traffike, which we ourselves, by means of the enviers of our Country's foreign Trade, were ready to yield them gratis, and as it were unsought and for nothing; yet if it may be rightly said, as undoubtedly it may be accounted, that England's trade is England's treasure, why should our gracious King and his people lose that so excellent a profit in a moment, which cost his Merchants so many years to compass, and so many hazards and charges to obtain and settle. A few privileges, and a little protection, a fair aspect and a gentle encouragement, from both these honourable assemblies, will quickly settle this Kingdom's Traffike, and not only preserve it in its present splendour, but also easily augment and enlarge it.

No doubt, as events had shown, it was extraordinarily difficult to find the right privileges to placate everybody. But there was a sense in which England's future treasure did lie in trade and traffic. And it was in this sense that the merchants as a group, although they sometimes worried about their prestige, were on the ascendant in English society. Civil war or no civil war, England was on the verge of its commercial revolution—a commercial revolution which would conquer empires in Asia and America, and defeat the power and wealth of capitalist Holland. In the ensuing expansion, this country not only laid the geographical basis for its Victorian glory, but accumulated the wealth and developed the skills which were to be the foundations for its industrial supremacy. That this process should have been achieved under the influence of a merchant group which was disunited, should not surprise us. The mechanisms of social change are not always as simple as we should like them to be.

Books for further reading

Robert Ashton, *The Crown and the Money Market 1603–1640* (1960).

P. J. Bowden, *The Wool Trade in Tudor and Stuart England* (1962).

K. N. Chaudhuri, *The English East India Company: The Study of an Early Joint-Stock Company, 1600–1640* (1965).

R. W. K. Hinton, *The Eastland Trade and the Common Weal in the Seventeenth Century* (1959).

W. Hyde Price, *The English Patents of Monopoly* (Boston, Mass., 1906).

P. McGrath (ed.), *Merchants and Merchandise in Seventeenth-Century Bristol* (1955).

T. C. Mendenhall, *The Shrewsbury Drapers and the Welsh Wool Trade in the XVI and XVII Centuries* (1953).

V. Pearl, *London and the Outbreak of the Puritan Revolution* (1961).

R. H. Tawney, *Business & Politics under James I: Lionel Cranfield as Merchant and Minister* (1958).

A. F. Upton, *Sir Arthur Ingram, c. 1565–1642. A Study of the Origins of an English Landed Family* (1961).

A. C. Wood, *A History of the Levant Company* (1935).

X

The Levellers

BRIAN MANNING

At the beginning of the Civil War both sides declared support for 'Mixed Monarchy'—the sharing of supreme power in the state between king, Lords, and Commons. By the end of the Civil War 'Mixed Monarchy' was rejected on the right wing of the king's party by Filmer and Hobbes, and also on the left wing of the parliament's party by the Levellers. The Levellers told the House of Commons

> that as the ground of the late war between the King and you, was a contention whether he or you should exercise the supreme power over us, so it's vain to expect a settlement of peace amongst us, until that point be clearly and justly determined . . .[1] It being indeed impossible for us to believe that it can consist either with the safety or freedom of the nation, to be governed either by three or two Supremes, especially where experience hath proved them so apt as to differ in their judgements concerning freedom or safety . . . And when as most of the oppressions of the Commonwealth have in all times been brought upon the people by the King and Lords, who nevertheless would be so equal in the supreme authority, as that there should be no redress of grievances, no provision for safety, but at their pleasure. For our parts, we profess ourselves so far from judging this to be consistent with freedom or safety, that we know no great cause wherefore we assisted you in the late wars, but in hope to be delivered by you from so intolerable, so destructive a bondage . . .

[1] 'To the Supream Authority of England . . .' (Petition of November 23, 1647). *Leveller Manifestoes of the Puritan Revolution*, ed. D. M. Wolfe (New York, 1944), p. 237.

But to our exceeding grief, we have observed that no sooner God vouchsafeth you victory . . . but . . . you . . . declared to all the world that you will not alter the ancient government, from that of King, Lords, and Commons: not once mentioning (in case of difference) which of them is supreme, but leaving that point (which was the chiefest cause of all our public differences, disturbances, wars and miseries) as uncertain as ever.[2]

The Levellers did not doubt that the outcome of the Civil War ought to be the establishment of the supremacy of the Commons over the king and the Lords.

For the Levellers, as for everybody in the seventeenth century, God was the source of justice. God made all men equal by nature; and he endowed men with reason, by which they could know God's justice. If one man assumed authority over other men, it would seem to be contrary to natural equality; and, since God ordained this equality, contrary to God's will, and therefore unjust. But this authority of one man over others became a just authority if the others consented to it, each one individually seeing by the light of his own reason a necessity for it; but if they did not consent to it, it was an unjust authority. The Levellers concluded that all just authority—all authority acceptable to God—must be derived from the consent of the people. They told the House of Commons:

That as we conceive all Governors and Magistrates, being the ordinance of man, before they be the ordinance of God, and no authority being of God, but what is erected by the mutual consent of a people: and seeing this Honourable House alone represents the people of this nation, that therefore no person whatsoever, be permitted to exercise any power or authority in this nation, who shall not clearly and confessedly, receive his power from this House, and be always accountable for the discharge of his trust, to the people in their representatives in Parliament.

The Levellers warned the Commons

That God expects justice from those before whose eyes he hath

[2] 'To the Right Honorable, The Commons of England . . .' (Petition of September 11, 1648), quoted in Wolfe, pp. 284-5.

destroyed an unjust generation: [if the Commons allow them-
selves] to depend upon the will of the King, and the Lords, which
were never chosen or betrusted by the people . . ., the invaluable
price of all the precious English blood spilt in the defence of
our freedoms against the King, shall be embezzled or lost; and
certainly God, the avenger of blood, will require it of the
obstructors of justice and freedom.[3]

The Levellers' supporters in the parliament's victorious New Model
Army declared:

This power of Commons in Parliament, is the thing against
which the King hath contended, and the people have defended
with their lives, and therefore ought now to be demanded as the
price of their blood.[4]

There was need for a new constitution because the old one was
discredited; and to be a just constitution it had to be derived from
the consent of the people. The Levellers composed a new constitution and called it 'An Agreement of the People', because it was to
be submitted for the people's approval, and to be made binding by
the people's consent. This constitution would have established the
supreme power of the House of Commons in the state. But the
Commons were to be supreme because they represented the people.
The power of the Commons was to be a trust from the people, and
the constitution was to ensure that the trust was performed to the
people's liking. The Levellers believed that, as no man was free from
sin, so any man with power would use it for his own selfish interest,
if he had the opportunity. Therefore they concluded that powers must
be so limited and divided that no one man or group of men had too
much of it. This was a central point in the thinking of the Levellers
and it was well illustrated by the reply of the leaders of the Levellers
to the allegation that,

if we were in power, we would bear ourselves as tyranically as

[3] 'To the Supream Authority of England . . .' (Petition of January, 1648)
quoted in Wolfe, pp. 264–5.
[4] 'The Case of the Armie truly stated . . .' (1647) quoted in Wolfe, pp.
212–13.

others have done: we confess indeed, that the experimental defections of so many men as have succeeded in authority, and the exceeding difference we have hitherto found in the same men in a low, and in an exalted condition, makes us even mistrust our own hearts, and hardly believe our own resolutions of the contrary. And therefore we have proposed such an establishment, as supposing men to be too flexible and yielding to worldly temptations, they should not yet have a means or opportunity either to injure particulars, or prejudice the public, without extreme hazard, and apparent danger to themselves.[5]

The Leveller party had its origins in the dismay of parliament's radical supporters in the Civil War at the arbitrary proceedings of the House of Commons in imprisoning people without trial and in refusing to receive petitions; and at the way in which members of parliament used their positions to enrich themselves at the expense of the public. This dismay led the Levellers to devise a constitution that would have not only defined but also limited the power of the Commons. Annual elections would have reduced the opportunities for members of parliament to have abused their power and would have made them responsible to the people. Thus in rejecting 'Mixed Monarchy', in which the power of the Commons was limited by the king and the Lords, the Levellers did not propose to set up an 'absolute power', but to limit the Commons by a written constitution based on the sovereignty of the people. Such a constitution could not be made by parliament because an act of parliament could always be altered or repealed by parliament; such a constitution could limit parliament only by being outside the control of parliament.

. . . Parliaments are to receive the extent of their power, and trust from those that betrust them; and therefore the people are to declare what their power and trust is, which is the intent of this Agreement. . . .[6]

[5] 'A Manifestation from Lieutenant-Col. John Lilburne, Mr. William Walwyn, Mr. Thomas Prince, and Mr. Richard Overton . . .' (1649) quoted in Wolfe, p. 394.

[6] 'An Agreement of the People . . .' (1647) quoted in Wolfe, p. 230.

The defeat of the king and the end of the Civil War presented both an urgent need to re-establish normal government and an unprecedented opportunity to remake the constitution. In an atmosphere of millenarian expectation that God had given victory to parliament and the New Model Army for some great purpose, and of excited speculation about the meaning of the recent struggle, the Levellers addressed the House of Commons:

> . . . You were chosen to work our deliverance, and to estate us in natural and just liberty agreeable to reason and common equity; for whatever our forefathers were, or whatever they did or suffered, or were enforced to yield unto, we are the men of the present age, and ought to be absolutely free from all kinds of exorbitances, molestations or arbitrary power, and you we chose to free us from all without exception or limitation . . .[7]

Thus the Levellers rejected history in the sense of tradition and precedent, and swept away the old constitution. But they adopted history in the sense of placing in the past the liberty for which they were now striving. Englishmen had been free before the Norman Conquest, so the Levellers believed; and they had lost their freedom at the hands of William the Conqueror, his barons, and his priests and lawyers. Ever since then Englishmen had been struggling against kings and lords and at last they had defeated them in the Civil War. Thus history had reached a turning-point—either Englishmen would go on to secure their freedom or they would relapse into slavery. The Levellers despaired of the House of Commons securing this freedom for the people: '. . . You have long time acted more like the House of Peers than the House of Commons.'[8] They were a House of Commons in name only, in practice they were a second House of Lords. So the Levellers turned to the New Model Army. There the influence of their ideas resulted in the formation of a Council of the Army consisting of officers and soldiers elected by the regiments. At a meeting in Putney church in the autumn of 1647 the Levellers urged the Council of the Army to adopt the 'Agreement of the People'. Wildman, speaking for the Levellers, argued:

[7] 'A Remonstrance of Many Thousand Citizens . . .' (1646) quoted in Wolfe, p. 114.
[8] *ibid.*, p. 120.

and a gentleman but two, or a poor man shall choose none?'[15] The Levellers declared that the 'charters' and 'pretended customs' of the boroughs (which kept municipal government and the parliamentary franchise in the hands of the richest citizens) were 'obstructions to the freedom and equality of the people's choice of their representatives'.[16] Hence the Levellers attached a great deal of importance to the redistribution of parliamentary seats in proportion to population. And on this point they gained the support of Cromwell and Ireton.

The qualification for the vote in the counties was the ownership of freehold land worth at least 40s. a year, but in the boroughs it varied widely from place to place. Many speakers in the Putney Debates pointed out that under this system a poor man sometimes had the vote while a rich man did not. And Cromwell and Ireton agreed that there was a case for extending the franchise to bring in all the well-to-do. But the Levellers demanded a much greater extension of the franchise, Wildman insisting:

> Every person in England hath as clear a right to elect his representatives as the greatest person in England. I conceive that's the undeniable maxim of government: that all government is in the free consent of the people. If [so], then upon that account there is no person that is under a just government, or hath justly his own, unless he by his own free consent be put under that government. This he cannot be unless he be consenting to it, and therefore, according to this maxim, there is never a person in England [but ought to have a voice in elections].[17]

Wildman and the Levellers took their stand on the laws of nature, which contained the 'principles and maxims of just government', and were accessible to everybody by the light of their natural reason. But Ireton was suspicious of a doctrine which allowed to each individual the right and duty to decide according to the light of his own reason and conscience what was just and what was unjust, to obey or to disobey an order according as he found it just or unjust.

---

[15] Woodhouse, p. 56.
[16] 'The Case of the Armie truly stated . . .' quoted in Wolfe, pp. 212–13.
[17] Woodhouse, pp. 65–6.

It was this doctrine that lay at the heart of the thinking of the Levellers and throughout the Putney Debates divided them from Ireton and the chief officers, to whom it seemed a doctrine of 'anarchy'. The Levellers based their demand for a wider franchise on the argument that no man was bound to obey a government or laws to which he had not given his consent through his representatives. Ireton claimed that no one had a right to elect the lawmakers 'that hath not a permanent fixed interest in this kingdom', that is, the owners of land and the freemen of corporations. 'All the main thing that I speak for, is because I would have an eye to property.'[18] The right to private property could not be derived from the law of nature, or the law of God, or the birthright of Englishmen, he argued, but only from the law, tradition, and constitution of the kingdom: reject them and property lost its sanction. The old constitution secured property because it was based on the ownership of property. Then Ireton made clear the fear underlying his rejection of the Leveller doctrine of a natural right to vote:

. . . If you admit any man that hath a breath and being, I did show you how this will destroy property. It may come to destroy property thus. You may have such men chosen, or at least the major part of them, [as have no local and permanent interest]. Why may not those men vote against all property?[19]

And Colonel Rich agreed with Ireton:

I confess [there is weight in] that objection that the Commissary-General last insisted upon; for you have five to one in this kingdom that have no permanent interest. Some men [have] ten, some twenty servants . . . If the master and servant shall be equal electors, then clearly those that have no interest in the kingdom will make it their interest to choose those that have no interest. It may happen, that the majority may by law . . . destroy property; there may be a law enacted, that there shall be an equality of goods and estate . . . I remember there were many workings and revolutions . . . in the Roman Senate; and there was never

18 *ibid.,* pp. 53–5, 57–8.
19 *ibid.,* p. 63.

a confusion that did appear . . . till the state came to know this
kind of distribution of election. That is how the people's voices
were bought and sold, and that by the poor; and thence it came
that he that was the richest man, and [a man] of some considerable
power among the soldiers, and one they resolved on, made
himself a perpetual dictator. And if we strain too far to avoid
monarchy in kings [let us take heed] that we do not call for
emperors to deliver us from more than one tyrant.[20]

And Ireton hammered home the point:

If you do extend the latitude [of the constitution so far] that any
man shall have a voice in election who has not that interest in this
kingdom that is permanent and fixed, who hath not that interest
upon which he may have his freedom in this kingdom without
dependence, you will put it into the hands of men to choose, [not]
of men [desirous] to preserve their liberty, [but of men] who will
give it away . . . If there be anything at all that is a foundation
of liberty it is this, that those who shall choose the law-makers
shall be men freed from dependence upon others.[21]

The Levellers had no intention of abolishing private property or
of redistributing wealth. Petty declared: '. . . I hope that they may
live to see the power of the King and the Lords thrown down, that
yet may live to see property preserved.'[22] The Leveller leaders
claimed 'that we never had it in our thoughts to level men's estates,
it being the utmost of our aim that the Commonwealth be reduced
to such a pass that every man may with as much security as may be
enjoy his property'.[23] And in the Agreement of the People they
inserted a clause denying to Parliament the power to 'level men's
estates, destroy property, or make all things common'.[24] The
Levellers claimed to speak for 'the poor and middle sort of people',
'men of inferior trading', the 'industrious people', such as the
clothiers, hatmakers, and soapboilers who figure prominently in

[20] *ibid.,* pp. 63–4.
[21] *ibid.,* p. 82.
[22] *ibid.,* p. 61.
[23] 'A Manifestation . . .' (1649) quoted in Wolfe, p. 391.
[24] 'An Agreement of the People . . .' (1648) quoted in Wolfe, pp. 300–1.

Lilburne's writings. Their references to farmers and labourers are infrequent in comparison with their references to the small master-craftsmen. The latter were the class from which the Levellers gained most of their support and the class whose aspirations the Levellers expressed. It was a class that owned property and prided itself on its independence, but it was a class which at the time of the Civil War was struggling to preserve its independence in face of the growth of capitalism.

The Levellers persistently attacked the rich. They attacked them for arrogance, uncharitableness, and oppression of the poor. They demanded that they restore the charitable donations and the common lands that they had stolen from the poor; and that they provide work and higher wages for the poor. They condemned the wealth of the government officials, whose large salaries were paid for by taxation that fell more heavily on 'the poor and middle sort' than on the rich; they condemned the wealth of the clergy, whose tithes were a heavy burden on the poor, especially the poor farmers; they condemned the wealth of the merchants, whose fortunes were the result of monopolies that excluded 'men of inferior trading' and ruined the master-craftsmen; they condemned the wealth of the lawyers, whose fees and tricks exhausted the purses of the small shopkeepers and tradesmen and gave victory in lawsuits to the parties with the longest purse. These men did not labour for their wealth 'with their hands, nor earn it with the sweat of their brows', but they extracted it from the fruits of the labour of 'the poor and men of middle quality', who as a result 'are scarcely able to subsist, pay rent, and maintain their families'.[25] The Levellers proposed to reduce the exploitation of the 'industrious people' by replacing the inequitable tax system established by parliament with a single tax 'by an equal rate in the pound upon every real and personal estate in the nation', and exemption for all persons 'not worth above £30'; by the abolition of tithes and of trading monopolies; and by reforms of the legal system which would have limited the profits of lawyers. But further, it was the possession of political power which gave opportunities for the rich—especially landlords—

[25] 'Englands Birth-Right Justified . . .' (1645) in *Tracts on Liberty in the Puritan Revolution*, ed. William Haller (New York, 1933), iii. 258–307.

to oppress the poor. As Rainborough protested in the Putney Debates:

> I am a poor man, therefore I must be oppressed: if I have no interest in the kingdom, I must suffer by all their laws be they right or wrong. Nay thus: a gentleman lives in a county and hath three or four lordships, as some men have (God knows how they got them); and when a Parliament is called he must be a Parliament-man; and it may be he sees some poor men, they live near this man, he can crush them—I have known an invasion to make sure he hath turned the poor men out of doors; and I would fain know whether the potency of [rich] men do not this, and so keep them under the greatest tyranny that was [ever] thought of in the world.[26]

The monopoly of political power by the rich enabled them to 'make hewers of wood and drawers of water' of the rest of the population.[27] It was for this reason that the Levellers wanted to reform the franchise—to abolish the monopoly of political power by the rich, just as they wanted to abolish the monopoly of trade by the big merchants, and of law by the lawyers, and of religious instruction by the clergy.

During the Putney Debates Colonel Rich proposed a compromise:

> I think that either of the extremes may be urged to inconveniency; that is, [that] men that have no interest as to estate should have no interest as to election [and that they should have an equal interest]. But there may be a more equitable division and distribution than that he that hath nothing should have an equal voice; and certainly there may be some other way thought of, that there may be a representative of the poor as well as the rich, and not to exclude all.[28]

And Petty, for the Levellers, agreed: 'The rich would very unwillingly be concluded by the poor. And there is as much reason that

[26] Woodhouse, p. 59.
[27] *ibid.*, p. 67.
[28] *ibid.*, pp. 63–4.

the rich should conclude the poor as the poor the rich—and indeed [that is] no reason [at all]. There should be an equal share in both.'[29] The Levellers wanted to balance the rich by giving the franchise to the 'middle sort', for whom a share in political power would enable them to preserve their economic independence. And the Levellers agreed to exclude from the franchise servants, labourers, and beggars —the people who could not be expected to act independently of the rich, their masters, employers, and benefactors. They did not advocate universal manhood suffrage, for they excluded more than a third of the population. Nevertheless the Levellers regarded the vote as the right of a man as a man, while Ireton regarded it as the right of a property owner as a property owner. Both Ireton and the Levellers wanted to preserve private property, but Ireton saw security of private property in the monopoly of political power by the property owners, while the Levellers saw the security for private property in the rights which rested on the consent of the people— property was one of the rights contained in the Agreement of the People. In practice the difference between Ireton and the Levellers was between a constitution which placed power in the hands of the gentry and merchants, and a constitution which placed power in the hands of the small property owners. And the difference is important, since more than half the population consisted of small property owners. In seventeenth-century England democracy could not be based on the wage-earners, whose conditions were close to beggary. The Levellers would have created a political system based on the mass of shopkeepers, craftsmen, and farmers; and that would have been indeed a democratic system.

The Levellers were an important factor in persuading the army to abolish the monarchy and the House of Lords and to set up the English Republic; but the army leaders successfully resisted those aspects of the Leveller programme which threatened the interests of the rich. The Levellers came near to gaining control of London but the army then seized control of the capital. The Levellers came near to winning control of the army, but most of the private soldiers were probably more concerned about their pay and conditions than about the reform of the constitution, and they were cowed by the shooting

[29] *ibid.,* p. 78.

of radical mutineers. Levellers were purged from the ranks and the army converted into a professional military force. The Leveller leaders were imprisoned and the army suppressed any movements in their favour. The upper-class republicans were satisfied with the establishment of a republic; the Independents and an influential section of the separatists were satisfied with the defeat of the Presbyterians; and the main body of Puritans was willing to see Cromwell and the army establish the 'godly discipline' at the point of the sword. And for the dissatisfied craftsmen, the Fifth Monarchists offered a rival revolutionary creed to that of the Levellers. Increasingly isolated, the Leveller leaders could still command the sympathy of the poorer citizens of London, but they could no longer convert sympathy into action. The Leveller leaders sacrificed their jobs, their families, and their liberty for the cause: there were no others to make the same sacrifices for them. The Cromwellian régime ensured that the English Revolution did not result in the destruction of the power of the gentry and the merchants, but without the support of the Levellers and the class they represented, it was doomed to be barren of the reforms that could have won it mass support.

Books for further reading

The Levellers' writings will be found in *Tracts on Liberty in the Puritan Revolution*, ed. William Haller (New York, 1933–4); *Leveller Manifestoes of the Puritan Revolution*, ed. D. M. Wolfe (1944); *The Leveller Tracts*, ed. William Haller and Godfrey Davies (New York, 1944). All have useful introductions.

The Putney Debates will be found, with much other material about the Levellers, in A. S. P. Woodhouse, *Puritanism and Liberty* (1938), with a most important introduction.

The fullest narrative of the Leveller movement and its influence is H. N. Brailsford, *The Levellers and the English Revolution*, ed. Christopher Hill (1961).

There are important articles by Christopher Hill, 'The Norman

Yoke', in *Puritanism and Revolution* (1958), and C. B. Macpherson, 'The Levellers: Franchise and Freedom', in *The Political Theory of Possessive Individualism* (1962). Macpherson shows that the Levellers did not advocate universal manhood suffrage but goes too far in denying that they were democrats and in implying that they were 'capitalists'.

There are other interesting studies of different aspects of Leveller thought by W. Schenk, *The Concern for Social Justice in the Puritan Revolution* (1948); D. B. Robertson, *The Religious Foundations of Leveller Democracy*, (New York, 1951); Perez Zagorin, *A History of Political Thought in the English Revolution*, (1954).

Select Bibliography

The best one-volume account of the Revolution, lively, learned and up-to-date, is Ivan Roots, *The Great Rebellion, 1642–1660* (Batsford, 1966), though its early chapters are heavily compressed. C. H. Firth, *Oliver Cromwell* (1900; World's Classics, 1953) is more than a biography and remains a classic. On a larger scale C. V. Wedgwood provides a most attractive, scholarly narrative in *The King's Peace, 1637–1641* and *The King's War, 1641–1647* (Collins, 1955 and 1958; further volumes to follow); her *Trial of Charles I* (Collins, 1964) should also be read. For a brief survey, Maurice Ashley, *Oliver Cromwell and the Puritan Revolution* (English U.P., 1958) is useful. The great standard works by S. R. Gardiner, *History of England, 1603–1642* (10 vols., 1883–4), and *History of the Great Civil War* (4 vols., 1893) and *History of the Commonwealth and Protectorate* (4 vols., 1903), are continued by C. H. Firth in *The Last Years of the Protectorate* (2 vols., 1910, repr. 1963) and brought down to 1660 by Godfrey Davies in *The Restoration of Charles II* (O.U.P., 1955).

Among more general works which place the Revolution in a broader context, the latest short introduction is G. E. Aylmer, *The Struggle for the Constitution, 1603–1689* (Blandford Press, 1963). Christopher [J. E. C.] Hill, *The Century of Revolution, 1603–1714* (Nelson, 1961) is thin on narrative but rich in stimulating commentary, whereas Godfrey Davies, *The Early Stuarts* (O.U.P., 2nd edn., 1959) is useful for factual information but meagre in interpretation. For the background to the revolution, on economic and social issues consult Charles Wilson, *England's Apprenticeship, 1603–1763* (Longmans, 1965) and B. E. Supple, *Commercial Crisis and Change in*

* Available in paperback, sometimes under different imprints.

England, 1600–1642 (C.U.P., 1959); on constitutional conflicts, Margaret Judson, *The Crisis of the Constitution, 1603–1645* (1949; repr. by Octagon Books, N.Y., 1964); and on the court and the office-holders G. E. Aylmer, *The King's Servants* (Longmans, 1961). For the religious issues see Christopher Hill, *The Economic Problems of the Church, from Whitgift to the Long Parliament* (O.U.P., 1956) and the reading list for Chapter 6.

Excerpts from all the chief contestants in the controversy over the rise of the gentry are edited by Lawrence Stone in ★*Social Change and Revolution in England, 1540–1640* (Longmans, 1965); see also P. A. M. Taylor (ed.), *The Origins of the English Civil War* (Heath, 1960). Stone's own massive work, *The Crisis of the Aristocracy, 1558–1641* (O.U.P., 1965; abridged ★O.U.P., 1967), is a major contribution to social history. A sociological approach is stimulatingly and sometimes provocatively presented by Peter Laslett in ★*The World We Have Lost* (Methuen, 1965). Christopher Hill, ★*Society and Puritanism* (Secker and Warburg, 1964) and *Intellectual Origins of the English Revolution* (O.U.P., 1965) attempt a radical new synthesis of religion and politics, society and ideas. P. Zagorin, *A History of Political Thought in the English Revolution* (Routledge, 1954) is the best short introduction to its important subject. Documents and useful commentaries are in J. P. Kenyon, ★*The Stuart Constitution* (C.U.P., 1966), but the older collections, S. R. Gardiner, *Constitutional Documents of the Puritan Revolution, 1625–1660* (O.U.P., 3rd edn., 1906, repr. 1958); G. W. Prothero, *Statutes and Constitutional Documents of the Reigns of Elizabeth and James I* (O.U.P., 4th edn., 1913, repr. 1954); J. R. Tanner, ★*Constitutional Documents of the Reign of James I* (C.U.P., 1930, repr. 1952) remain of value.

The period is disappointingly served by biographies, but one may recommend J. P. Kenyon, ★*The Stuarts* (Batsford, 1958); D. H. Wilson, *James VI and I* (Cape, 1956); H. R. Trevor-Roper, ★*Archbishop Laud* (Macmillan, 2nd ed., 1962); C. V. Wedgwood, ★*Thomas Wentworth, First Earl of Strafford* (Cape, 1961); Maurice Ashley, ★*The Greatness of Oliver Cromwell* (Hodder & Stoughton, 1957); Pauline Gregg, *Freeborn John* [Lilburne] (Harrap, 1961). B. H. G. Wormald, *Clarendon* (C.U.P., 1951) and J. H. Hexter, *The*

Reign of King Pym (Harvard U.P., 1941) are not biographies but both illuminate important aspects of the revolution.

Many of the above books have good bibliographies; particularly helpful are those in Roots, *The Great Rebellion*; Davies, *The Early Stuarts*; Kenyon, *The Stuart Constitution*; and Stone, *Social Change and Revolution.*

Index

Index